Aquafaba

Also by Zsu Dever

Vegan Bowls

Everyday Vegan Eats

Aquafaba

Sweet and Savory Vegan Recipes
Made Egg-Free with the Magic of Bean Water

Zsu Dever

Foreword by Goose Wohlt

VEGAN HERITAGE PRESS, LLC

Woodstock • Virginia

ISBN: 978-1-941252-27-7

First Edition, October 2016

10 9 8 7 6 5 4 3 2

Vegan Heritage Press, LLC books are available at quantity discounts. For information, please visit our website at www.veganheritagepress.com or write the publisher at Vegan Heritage Press, P.O. Box 628, Woodstock, VA 22664-0628.

Library of Congress Cataloging-in-Publication Data

Name: Dever, Zsu, 1972-
Title: Aquafaba : sweet and savory vegan recipes made egg-free with the
    magic of bean water / Zsu Dever.
Description: Woodstock, Virginia : Vegan Heritage Press, 2016.
Identifiers: LCCN 2016029483 (print) | LCCN 2016034832 (ebook) | ISBN
    9781941252277 (paperback) | ISBN 9781941252284 (epub) | ISBN 9781941252291
    (prc)
Subjects: LCSH: Vegan cooking. | Vegetable juices. | Tofu. | BISAC: COOKING /
    Health & Healing / Allergy. | COOKING / Vegetarian & Vegan. | LCGFT:
    Cookbooks.
Classification: LCC TX837 .D378 2016 (print) | LCC TX837 (ebook) | DDC
    641.5/636--dc23

Photo credits: Cover and interior photos by Zsu Dever.

Vegan Heritage Press, LLC books are distributed by Andrews McMeel Publishing.

Printed in the United States of America

DEDICATION

For the hens, first and foremost.

And for my incredible husband,
whose support keeps me moving.

CONTENTS

FOREWORD

||||||||||||||||||||||||||||||

Throughout history, the egg has been associated with rebirth, renewal, and creation. For many, breaking the nightly fast as the sun rises with a meal of eggs is a daily ritual. Images of cooking eggs permeate our cultural consciousness and media. For vegans, however, the positive symbolism traditionally associated with eggs has been replaced with a reminder of the harsh and brutal reality of animal agriculture. Humans are a creative bunch, and nowhere is that more apparent than in the collection of alternatives those on egg-restricted diets have devised in order to replicate the culinary properties of eggs.

Existing egg substitutes run the gamut from whole foods like bananas and applesauce to commercial mixes based on refined starches or ground nuts and seeds. More recently, we are seeing mixes of proteins, starches, and vegetable gums to cover more applications and reduce some of the limitations of existing substitutes. These combinations trade the simplicity of whole foods for a more accurate emulation of egg properties, but even the best mixes fall short in several key areas like egg-white foams on cocktails or the pillowy white foam of the inimitable egg-based meringue.

In early 2015, I was asked to make meringues for my mother's vegan seder. After an Internet search for vegan meringues turned up few recipes, I spent a few weeks trying what I could to make foams from random kitchen and molecular gastronomy ingredients. Eventually, I had all but settled on a meringue mostly based on a commercial starchy egg replacer and made with a specific ratio of water, sugar, and baking temperature. The texture of the meringue was so-so, and the taste was reminiscent of cardboard, but at least the sugar masked it enough to make it edible. That's when I heard about an online video in which a pair of French chefs used the foam made from a can of chickpeas and chocolate to make a chilled mousse. I wondered if maybe the foam they were using would be strong enough to work in the recipe I had created.

After opening a can of chickpeas and pouring the slimy liquid through a fine tea strainer into a kitchen stand mixer bowl, I flicked on the power to see what would happen. Moments later, out of this goopy waste product a pillowy, dense foam arose, exactly like you might expect from egg whites. Encouraged by this odd alchemical combination of magic and science unfolding in the bowl, I decided it would be prudent to keep all other variables the same and tried the same sugar, liquid, and heat from previous trials. With the addition of the sugar, the foam gained strength and took on the characteristic sheen of egg-based meringues. I popped a few amorphous blobs of meringue in the oven to see what would happen overnight. The next morning, when the oven door was opened, there they were. They had the very same texture and taste that I remembered from egg-white meringues and were made with only two ingredients! Here was a nearly perfect meringue substitute without any refined starches, gums, proteins, leavening agents, or fancy "mod" ingredients. Out of habit, I snapped a picture and posted to the Facebook group "What Fat Vegans Eat," a vegan food-centered group with almost 35,000 members at the time.

As winter gave way to spring in March 2015, the proverbial vegan egg cracked open to the steadily growing sound of people biting into meringues, pavlovas, and macarons worldwide. The nest in which this all took place was a new Facebook group *Vegan Meringues – Hits and Misses!* The group was formed in order to tease out why some were having great success replicating the meringue while others were failing.

One of the founding ideas of this new group was that by sharing what failed along with what worked, we could learn from the mistakes of others and build upon them instead of reproducing the same failures over and over, wasting time and ingredients. This, combined with global accessibility to bean-cooking liquid, meant that traditional egg-based recipes were suddenly available to a large number of people, without the need for obscure ingredients like refined starches or vegetable gums. Kitchens across the globe turned out new and exciting desserts, and delicious recreations of culturally significant dishes (like pavlovas) that many had given up hope of having again finally became possible.

It wasn't just new discoveries and recipes that popped up in the group in those first few weeks. There was also a proliferation of names for the new liquid. There simply was no existing word for the liquid, leaving the authors of new posts to decide how to refer to the new liquid using names like "l'egg," "bean juice," "bean brine," and "chickpea liquid." The group eventually settled on "aquafaba," which is a mashup of Latin for "water" and Latin for "bean," but which also carries with it connotations of being fabulous and representing the family of pulses, fabacaea. Not only was a completely new word born, but with it, this strong sense of community and collaboration.

The fledging of aquafaba took the form of a proliferation of blog posts with recipes for marshmallows, cookies, cakes, mayonnaise, Italian meringue buttercream icing, butter, cheese, and much, much more. With the release of commercial products and articles in major news outlets like the *New York Times, Boston Globe,* and the *Guardian,* aquafaba has spread its wings and taken flight into a life of its own.

An aquafaba book is long overdue, and in a fitting coincidence, this book is being released in the year that has been declared by the United Nations as the International Year of Pulses. If you search for aquafaba online, you will see thousands of pages of results. The Facebook groups and aquafaba community provide welcome support to newcomers. There are documents in the Facebook groups with collections of popular recipes, and there are hundreds of blog posts about aquafaba. It can be a bit overwhelming for someone just learning about aquafaba and sometimes confusing as to how to get started. Some of the information online is misleading or wrong and some is very useful, but there hasn't been any single place to go to learn what aquafaba is, how to use it, and the pitfalls that you might encounter following recipes with it. That's what makes this book so wonderful.

Zsu Dever's *Aquafaba* takes the reader by the hand on a clear journey through some of the major places in the aquafaba landscape, exploring both sweet and savory recipes and providing detailed information about how to make your own at home. It is everything one might need to get started working with aquafaba and provides enough information for those looking to explore some of the more subtle aspects of it. This is really more than just a cookbook; it's a primer for aquafaba that captures the essence of the community in its pages and even provides guidance on what to do with all those leftover chickpeas that you will inevitably generate in your own explorations.

Hopefully, this book will encourage you to join the growing community of explorers and share what you learn from aquafaba on its continued flight through kitchens worldwide. I hope you enjoy this aquafaba compendium as much as I do.

GOOSE WOHLT
Muncie, Indiana

INTRODUCTION
||||||||||||||||||||||||||||||||||||||||||||

Aquafaba. The online community has been on fire since March 2015, when the news broke that someone had discovered a way to mimic the properties of egg whites using the liquid from a can of chickpeas. The by-product of cooking dried legumes can actually be turned into meringues and other foods that vegans have avoided for years. People started experimenting with aquafaba to see just how far the bean brine could be pushed into mimicking the behavior of eggs. There were aquafaba macarons popping up, angel food cake trials and tribulations, cookies made with aquafaba, and the list goes on; if a recipe had previously been made with eggs, you can bet someone somewhere tried substituting aquafaba in the recipes—some with surprising success.

My first foray using aquafaba was making the super-easy Meringue Cookies. I was stunned at how beautifully aquafaba went from being an amber-colored viscous liquid to a shiny, pure white foam that was thick but light. After I tasted the airy cookies I was immediately transported back to my childhood when we would buy them at the local bakery on special occasions. Of course, aquafaba continues to astound me, but that first experience with it was simply amazing. It really is something you have to experience firsthand.

In addition to the obvious benefits that aquafaba brings to the vegan community, it also provides the very same benefits to anyone allergic to eggs or dairy, because aquafaba performs well in certain dairy-based recipes, such as whipped cream and cheese.

What exactly is aquafaba? It is nothing more than the cooking water from legumes. Those legumes can be anything, even peas and lentils, but the general consensus is that the darker the bean, the stronger the flavor and color of the brine. That stronger flavor can be distinguished in some applications; therefore, the best beans to use are the lighter-colored chickpeas, lima beans, and cannellinis. As far as the science goes, we have very little information. We think some properties of the beans (carbohydrates and protein) leech into the cooking liquid and that these ingredients, with the proper consistency, mimic certain qualities of eggs. It is also thought that aquafaba can act in some respects like egg yolks and in others as egg whites. However, aquafaba does not act as one or the other exclusively.

As miraculous as aquafaba may be, it does have some limitations. Eggs consist of the whites and the yolks. The whites of eggs are made up of mostly water (about 90 percent) and protein (about 10 percent). Although the whites are made mostly of water, the other 10 percent contains about half of the protein of the complete egg. The purpose of whites in the egg is to protect the yolk and, if the egg becomes fertilized, to supply nutrition to the growing chick. Egg yolks are one of the few single cells that are visible to the human eye. Upon fertilization, the yolk is the food source for the growing chick. About half the protein in the egg is supplied by the yolk. It is also the source of all the fat in the egg.

While we don't yet have a chemical analysis of aquafaba, there are a few things we can discern. Since legumes consist mostly of carbohydrates and protein, it seems likely that the brine that the beans are cooked in contains those same properties. Therefore, aquafaba is made up of mostly carbohydrates, protein, and water, whereas eggs consist of fat, protein, and water. The amount of protein and the difference between carbohydrates and fat are most likely the cause of the limitations of cooking with aquafaba. The brine is also full of soap-like components called saponins, which act to hold the structure of the brine foam. So, while it makes awesome meringue and macaron cookies, aquafaba by itself will not create custards, éclairs, or omelets. Although there are a few ways to help aquafaba out (by adding starches, stabilizers, proteins, and other ingredients, for example), unlike eggs, aquafaba is not a stand-alone ingredient.

Aquafaba is undoubtedly one of the most fantastic culinary discoveries of the decade, but who was the first to look at the liquid that most of us dump down the drain as liquid gold? This question planted the seed that would later grow into a workable meringue recipe. According to Aquafaba.com, a few years went by before Miyoko Schinner shared her 2012 experiments using flaxseed mucilage to make vegan meringue cookies. This caused others to expand their ideas of what could be used as vegan egg whites. Then, in 2014, Joël Roessel (a French tenor singer who experimented with molecular gastronomy) discovered that the brine of chickpeas could be whipped into a foam. A mere few months later, a French video was uploaded that used the foam to make a chocolate mousse dessert. That video inspired Goose Wohlt, a U.S. software engineer who had already been experimenting with hydrocolloids, to continue experimenting and create a stable meringue, using only chickpea brine and sugar. In fact, it was Goose who eventually named the magical ingredient "aquafaba," which is a combination of the Latin root words for "water" and "bean," and the name stuck.

At the beginning of March 2015, Goose shared his discovery on the Facebook page What Fat Vegans Eat and it was like an explosion in the vegan community. (I remember where I was when this news hit!) In fact, there are now two separate Facebook communities of chefs and home cooks who share their experiences and recipes with the world: Meringue végane – C'est moi qui l'ai faite! (hosted in French by Joël Roessel) and Vegan Meringue – Hits and Misses! (hosted in English by Rebecca August). Of course, now the groups discuss far more than just meringues! The groups are true online communities of dedicated individuals who love to share what they have discovered, and you are encouraged to join and share in the ever evolving achievements of aquafaba. Both Joël and Goose, along with the students, are regular contributors in the communities.

This book contains aquafaba recipes that range from easy to more complex. If aquafaba is brand new to you (or even if you have been using aquafaba for a while), start with the recipe on how to make aquafaba from dried beans and then read up on how to whip it properly. Because the consistency of the meringue is so important, everyone should run with that recipe first. Then, if you are new to the ingredient, start with something simple to make like Meringue Cookies or Featherlight Chocolate Mousse. Once you get your bearings, you can create Lemon Meringue Pie, Marshmallows, and even light and tender Italian Meatballs. Since aquafaba is more than just meringue, there are also recipes that use it as an emulsifier in dressings, sauces, and cheese. Aquafaba, in combination with higher-protein ingredients, can also be made into egg-like dishes such as Frittata and quiches. This book also covers candy, cake, whipped topping, bread, doughnuts, and even ice cream.

Once you have a batch of chickpeas cooked, I give you some creative ways to utilize the versatile bean in recipes such as Shiro Wot, an Ethiopian stew; Pulled Chickpea Seitan Roast; Roasted Chickpeas Four Ways; and Chickpea Gulyás. You won't have any problems figuring out what to do with leftover beans.

In spite of some limitations, there is no denying that aquafaba is a revolutionary discovery. This must be what Jack was talking about when he bought those magic beans; it has just taken us some time to uncover this truly magical application of the humble legume.

AN AQUAFABA PRIMER

What It Is
How to Make It
How to Whip It
How to Use It
How to Store It

Aquafaba is the liquid produced during the process of cooking beans. The raw ingredient can be aquired by draining a can of beans; however, the best aquafaba is homemade and the best beans to use are chickpeas.

Homemade aquafaba is stronger, more stable, tastes less of legumes, and goes much further in cooking than aquafaba from canned beans or other types of beans. In fact, while some canned chickpeas or beans will leave a slight lingering taste of legumes, homemade aquafaba is completely indiscernible in cooking. Since homemade chickpea aquafaba is the best by far, my recipes call for home-made exclusively. In addition to the above reasons, making your own aquafaba is important for two other reasons as well. First, making your own aquafaba yields a product that is consistent in strength and viscosity and will produce the most accurate results in the recipes. Second, homemade aquafaba is economical because it yields more aquafaba than you get from a can. Dried beans are also less expensive than canned beans.

You can begin experimenting with aquafaba by using canned chickpeas, but once you discover how wonderful aquafaba is, you will want to make your own. The easiest way is to cook your chickpeas in a slow cooker for eight to nine hours; I cook mine overnight.

TO MAKE YOUR OWN AQUAFABA

As I mentioned earlier, making aquafaba at home is the best way to go. You can use any dried chickpeas, but be aware that different brands, even different cooking methods, will result in a slightly different amount of aquafaba. After you cook up a batch, check the Aquafaba Yield Guide (page 3) to make sure you have the proper concentration.

2 cups chickpeas, picked over, rinsed, and drained
5 1/2 cups water
2 (1 x 1-inch) pieces kombu

Add the chickpeas, water, and kombu to a slow cooker. Cook on low for 8 to 9 hours, or until the chickpeas are tender. Remove and discard the kombu. Drain the chickpeas, strain them (if needed), and store the aquafaba as desired; store the chickpeas separately, as desired. Make sure your aquafaba is free of bean particles, as they might interfere with the whipping.

Note: Kombu is an essential ingredient in making aquafaba from home-cooked beans as it releases minerals that help soften the beans and make the aquafaba more viscous. Since kombu contains several essential minerals—such as calcium, iron, and iodine—it is beneficial in more ways than one.

Makes 2 1/2 to 2 3/4 cups aquafaba (and 6 cups cooked chickpeas)

GF, NF, SF

OTHER COOKING METHODS

Stove-top cooking method: Cook the beans in 8 cups water over low heat for 4 hours. Add more water as needed.

Pressure cooking: I do not recommend pressure-cooking the beans. Although pressure-cooking will make aquafaba, it will not be strong straight out of the cooker for use in the recipes in this book.

As not all chickpeas are created equal, not all slow cookers heat the same, using the stove-top method will yield various amounts of aquafaba, and unforeseen environmental occurrences have a way of messing with the yield of aquafaba, I have created guidelines to produce aquafaba with the most consistent results.

Aquafaba Yield Guide

Due to the variables of stove temperature, age of the beans, and other factors, use this guide to monitor your yields. After draining the aquafaba from the beans, follow these instructions:

- If your yield of aquafaba is more than 2 2/3 cups and you have 6 cups of well-cooked (but not overcooked) chickpeas, reduce the liquid over medium heat in a medium saucepan until the level reaches 2 2/3 cups.

- If your yield of aquafaba is less than 2 1/2 cups, but you have 5 3/4 to 6 cups of well-cooked (but not overcooked) chickpeas, add water until the level reaches 2 1/2 cups.

- If your yield of aquafaba is less than 2 1/2 cups, but you have less than 5 3/4 cups of well-cooked (but not overcooked) chickpeas, leave the aquafaba as is.

- If your beans are not cooked well, continue to cook for another hour until they are tender and follow the above guidelines.

MAKING REDUCED AQUAFABA

In certain recipes, the aquafaba needs to be reduced to minimize the water content. In recipes such as the Sweet Whipped Topping (page 88) and Toom Sauce (page 17), the Reduced Aquafaba helps the ingredients emulsify better and stabilizes the structure of the recipe.

Reduced Aquafaba: Add 1 cup aquafaba to a medium saucepan. Bring it to a boil and reduce it to a simmer over medium heat. Cook the aquafaba until it has reduced by half. Chill the aquafaba in the refrigerator until it is thick and cold. If you are doubling the recipe, increase the pan size as the aquafaba can boil over.

Makes 1/2 cup

AQUAFABA FROM CANNED BEANS

While I strongly encourage you to cook your own chickpeas to make aquafaba, there will be times when you will simply need it and need it fast. On those occasions, drain the liquid from a can of chickpeas (salted beans will yield a salty aquafaba), add it to a measuring cup, note the amount, transfer it to a medium saucepan, and cook to reduce it by one-third.

Cool the aquafaba before using. Once it is cool, canned (as well as homemade) aquafaba will thicken and congeal. The viscosity, while a rough estimate of the strength of aquafaba, is not an exact determination, so the thickness of your aquafaba does not indicate how strong it is. For instance, when warm, aquafaba is very thin; however, it is just as effective as when it is cool. Your recipe is what actually determines whether you will need the aquafaba cool, room temperature, or warm.

Aquafaba can be used in a one-to-one ratio for egg whites (2 tablespoons aquafaba for 1 large egg white); however, this equation will not work in all applications. Because aquafaba is inherently different from eggs, it will not act the same in all recipes. Although aquafaba does mimic some properties (such as foaming and emulsifying), it cannot act the same in other ways (such as coagulating or leavening). Following the recipes in this book is your first and best way to get to know the strengths and limitations of aquafaba.

STORAGE

After cooking your chickpeas, drain the aquafaba and store it in an airtight container in the refrigerator or freeze it in ice cube trays, which you then pop into an airtight container (remember to always label and date stored food). As for the chickpeas, they can be refrigerated or frozen for future use as well. Layer them on a large baking sheet and freeze them. Once they are completely frozen, pop them into an airtight container in the freezer and, when needed, remove as many as you like. Alternatively, if you will be using your chickpeas within seven days, transfer them to quart jars and cover the chickpeas with fresh water or leave them bare (something I have come to do; stored in an airtight container, the beans keep just as long as if stored in water).

Store your aquafaba in an airtight container (mason jars are great) for five to seven days in the refrigerator, or up to three months in the freezer, again in an airtight container.

Smell your aquafaba before each use; if it smells like spoiled beans, toss it. Always store the aquafaba in the refrigerator to ensure the longest shelf life.

WHIPPING AQUAFABA

SOFT, FIRM, AND STIFF PEAKS

Once you have aquafaba, this is the recipe to start with. If you have never seen the power of aquafaba or if you have no experience with egg whites, this is a great recipe to play around with. Consider this a quick tutorial on aquafaba peaks and textures. This is the best way to familiarize yourself with the all-important soft, firm, and stiff peaks. The more experience you have with whipping aquafaba, the more successful the recipes in this book will be. (See photo on page 6.)

1/2 cup aquafaba
1/2 teaspoon cream of tartar
2 tablespoons granulated organic sugar

Soft Peaks in 4 Minutes: Add the aquafaba and cream of tartar to the bowl of a stand mixer. Use a whisk or the balloon whip attachment to hand-whip the aquafaba for 10 seconds. Add the balloon whip to the machine or use a hand mixer to whip the aquafaba for 4 minutes at medium-low speed; this will begin to whip the aquafaba without taxing your machine. Stop the machine, remove the whip, dip it into the aquafaba and pull the whip straight up. Turn the whip upside down and notice the peaks that are formed: they are soft and will melt back into the aquafaba. These are soft peaks.

Firm Peaks in 9 to 10 Minutes: Increase the speed to medium-high speed and continue to whip the aquafaba for 5 to 6 minutes, or until you repeat the peak test and, after lifting the whip straight out of the aquafaba and turning the whip upside down, a peak forms that will fall over into the shape of a bird beak. These are firm peaks.

Stiff Peaks in 13 to 25 Minutes: Continue to whip on medium-high speed and add the sugar, 1 tablespoon at a time, over the span of 1 minute. Continue to beat for another 3 to 4 minutes. The aquafaba foam will now begin climbing the sides of the bowl and will begin to look dry. Repeating the peak test will now result in a peak on the whip that will stand straight up and not fall over at all. The foam at this point is thick and heavy, and it will begin to separate into firm pieces. It has reached the stiff peaks stage. Unlike egg whites, you cannot overwhip aquafaba, so when in doubt, continue to beat it until you have a meringue that will look and behave as described. Since this is a learning meringue, it is best to continue to beat it for up to 25 minutes so you can be sure you know what stiff peaks are. The firmness of your meringue will be critical in any recipe.

Note: The amount of time you whip your aquafaba will depend on how concentrated it is, how much of it there is, whether it is whipped with sugar, and whether there is cream of tartar in the recipe. Each recipe in this book takes all those factors into account; therefore, the timing for whipping aquafaba might be slightly different in each recipe. Pay attention to the consistency called for in each recipe.

Aquafaba Tips and Tricks

- Make sure your bowl and whip or whisk are impeccably clean. Any oil or fat will interfere with developing the foam. Plastic bowls hold onto fats and are therefore not recommended for use.

- Use the cream of tartar because it helps stabilize the foam.

- Make sure your whip is able to reach the aquafaba. If it cannot, add more aquafaba or manually whip the aquafaba until the balloon whip can reach.

- Whipping smaller or larger amounts of aquafaba than specified in recipes will take longer to whip than as directed.

- Whipping at slower speed will increase the time it takes to achieve firm or stiff peaks.

- If adding liquid fat to the whipped aquafaba, the aquafaba will completely break down and deflate unless the foam is at stiff peaks and the fat is added in a very slow, steady stream.

- Adding alcohol-based extracts to a meringue will deflate it. Add extracts that do not contain alcohol and only add them once the meringue is stable at stiff peaks.

- Adding hot liquids (such as melted coconut oil) will deflate the meringue to a certain extent, sometimes completely. Pay attention to the temperature, especially when using oil.

- Whipped meringue that has been deflated will rise in an oven set around 300°F when combined with a starch and protein. For this reason, it is a normal occurrence to be instructed in recipes to deflate the meringue before baking.

CONVENIENT RECIPE NOTATIONS

The recipes in this book come with helpful notations designed to help you manage your food sensitivities, save time, and make easy ingredient substitutions.

GF (Gluten-Free): These recipes are gluten-free with no substitution required.

GFO (Gluten-Free Option): These recipes are gluten-free with the indicated modifications.

NF (Nut-Free): These recipes are nut-free with no substitution required.

NFO (Nut-Free Option): These recipes are nut-free with the indicated modifications.

SF (Soy-Free): These recipes are soy-free with no substitution required.

SFO (Soy-Free Option): These recipes are soy-free with the indicated modifications.

Substitutions: The recipes also indicate ingredient substitutions where appropriate and possible.

In the next chapter, you will find aquafaba recipes for condiments such as dressings, sauces, and butter. In other chapters you will find a few basic recipes to help complete aquafaba recipes in the book, such as pie crusts, a honey substitute, and yogurt. Some recipes are there for your convenience and others are key for aquafaba recipes.

CONDIMENTS

One of the most fantastic properties of aquafaba is its emulsifying ability. This chapter highlights that component quite clearly. You can use aquafaba to make anything from butter to mayonnaise to cheese.

BUTTER

The first to develop a homemade vegan butter were trailblazers Mikoyo Schinner and Skye Michael Conroy, who led the charge using coconut oil. Bryanna Clark Grogan made her vegan Buttah using deodorized cocoa butter. Nina of PlantePusherne.dk first thought of making vegan butter using aquafaba, and we are all very pleased she made the connection. Thank you, Nina! As with all the recipes in this book, use refined coconut oil, which has very little to no coconut flavor; otherwise, your butter will have a coconut taste. You can use this butter in most of the recipes in this book. Any recipe that has been tested with this butter is so marked.

> 1/2 cup aquafaba
> 1/2 cup unsweetened plain soymilk or Homemade Almond Milk (page 15)
> 1/2 teaspoon sea salt
> 1/4 teaspoon granulated organic sugar
> 1/4 teaspoon vegan lactic acid, or 1 teaspoon plain Yogurt (page 18), or 1 teaspoon plain unsweetened store-bought soy or almond nondairy yogurt
> Large pinch turmeric
> 1/2 cup plus 1 tablespoon refined coconut oil
> 7 tablespoons canola or other neutral oil

1. Add the aquafaba, milk, salt, sugar, lactic acid, and turmeric to a medium saucepan. Bring the mixture to a boil and reduce to a simmer over medium heat, stirring constantly; the milk will foam up. Cook until the mixture has reduced to 1/2 cup. Cool the mixture to room temperature.

2. Completely melt the coconut oil and combine it with the canola oil; set this aside to come to room temperature.

3. Add the room-temperature milk mixture to a blender or wide-mouth jar large enough for an immersion blender. Process for 20 seconds. With the machine running (medium speed on a standard blender), add the oil mixture to the blender or jar in a slow, steady stream to emulsify the mixture. If using an immersion blender, move the stick up and down to help the oil emulsify. Increase the speed on a standard blender to medium-high after half of the oil has been added. The butter should be smooth and creamy.

4. Transfer the butter to silicone ice cube molds, if desired, and chill until very firm, about 4 hours. If you made the butter in a jar, add a lid and refrigerate the jar to firm up. The butter changes texture over time, going from very creamy to very dense.

Makes about 1 1/2 cups

GF, NF, SF

Cocoa Butter-Based Variation: Use 1/2 cup (105 grams) deodorized fair-trade cocoa butter, melted, instead of the coconut oil. Increase the canola or other neutral oil to 1/2 cup.

EVERYDAY CHEESE

Aquafaba is not the first thing that comes to mind when making cheese, so it was surprising when I first came across Lacey Siomos's Mozzarella Aquafaba Cheese. She made the emulsification connection when she watched Jay Astafa add lecithin to his vegan cheese. Skye Michael Conroy also talks of emulsification in his cheese recipes, so Lacey's assumption was astute. (To see more about Lacey and her recipes, visit her blog at AvocadosandAles.com.) The flavor of my cheese depends on the flavor of the yogurt that you use. Use a mildly tangy yogurt, if possible. This cheese comes together fast and is ready for use as soon as it sets, usually in a few hours. It melts and even makes great pizza and grilled cheese.

> 3/4 cup aquafaba
> 4 teaspoons agar powder
> 1 1/2 teaspoons chickpea or white miso
> 1 tablespoon plus 1 1/2 teaspoons nutritional yeast flakes
> 1 tablespoon tapioca starch
> 1 1/4 teaspoons sea salt
> 3/4 cup unsweetened plain soymilk or Homemade Almond Milk (page 15), divided
> 3 tablespoons refined coconut oil, melted
> 1/2 cup plus 1 tablespoon Yogurt (page 18) or plain unsweetened store-bought soy or almond
>   nondairy yogurt

1. Combine the aquafaba and agar in a medium saucepan and set aside for 3 minutes to thicken. Combine the miso, nutritional yeast, tapioca starch, and salt in a small container and set aside. Combine 1/4 cup of the milk with the coconut oil.

2. Heat the agar mixture over medium heat and use a whisk to mix well. Bring the mixture to a boil and cook for 1 minute. While whisking vigorously, add the milk-oil mixture in a slow, steady stream. Add the nutritional yeast mixture and whisk until very smooth. Whisk in the remaining 1/2 cup milk slowly and bring the mixture back to simmer over medium heat. Cook the cheese for 5 minutes; the cheese should reach 195°F. Stir it constantly to avoid scorching. Whisk in the yogurt and return the cheese to a simmer.

3. While the cheese is still hot, transfer it to a 2 1/2-cup heat-proof container. Cool the cheese at room temperature. Chill the cheese in the refrigerator at least 6 hours to firm up. Store it in an airtight container for up to 2 weeks.

Makes about 2 1/4 cups

GF, NF, SF

CREAM CHEESE

This is a tangy, thick cream cheese. If you'd like it extra-firm, increase the coconut oil to 1/4 cup. It also helps to drain your yogurt using a linen or hemp nut bag to retain most of the curds from the yogurt and get rid of as much whey as possible. For a soy-free version, use Almond-Cashew Yogurt (page 19) and soy-free vegan butter.

    2 tablespoons aquafaba, room temperature
    3 tablespoons refined coconut oil, melted
    3 tablespoons nondairy butter, melted
    1 1/2 teaspoons granulated organic sugar
    1/4 teaspoon sea salt
    1 cup mild Yogurt (page 18), drained for 24 hours

1. Add the aquafaba to a food processor. With the machine running, add the coconut oil in a slow, steady stream. (It will take 1 tablespoon of oil being added before the blade of the processor will begin to blend all the ingredients; this is normal.) Add the butter in a slow, steady stream. Add the sugar and salt and continue to process for 20 more seconds. Remove the processor's lid and add the yogurt.

2. Process the cream cheese until very smooth and silky. Transfer it to an airtight container and allow it to firm up for 24 hours before using. The cream cheese will keep in an airtight container in the refrigerator for 10 to 14 days.

Makes about 1 1/2 cups

GF, NF, SFO

COUNTRY-STYLE AGED SHARP CHEESE

The key to this cheese is using mild-tasting yogurt (so the final cheese is not overwhelming) and well-drained yogurt. The yogurt is ready when it is thick enough to form into a ball. This cheese is comparable to the aged block cheeses that are available commercially. After you make it once, consider making two or three blocks at a time, perhaps with the addition of some fresh herbs, such as chives or basil. The cheese takes about four days to make, but it's mostly hands-off time. Use Almond-Cashew Yogurt (page 19) for a soy-free version.

1/4 cup aquafaba
2 tablespoons refined coconut oil, just melted and at room temperature
2 teaspoons nutritional yeast flakes
2 teaspoons chickpea or white miso
1/2 teaspoon sea salt
1 cup mild Yogurt (page 18)

1. Add the aquafaba to a heat-proof bowl large enough to sit over a saucepan of simmering water (this creates a double boiler). Heat the aquafaba until it is warm and add the coconut oil slowly while whisking the aquafaba. Whisk in the nutritional yeast, miso, and salt. Whisk well to combine. Whisk in the yogurt until a smooth consistency is reached. Cook the cheese, stirring often, until it is warmer than 140°F, about 4 minutes.

2. Transfer the cheese to a 2-cup silicone mold or container lined with parchment paper. Chill the cheese in the refrigerator to firm up for at least 8 hours.

3. Remove the cheese from the mold and place it on parchment paper (if not using parchment in the previous step). Form the cheese into a disk about 1-inch thick. Transfer the cheese and the parchment paper to a dehydrator or a baking sheet placed inside a box. Using only the fan (no heat) of the dehydrator, dry the cheese for about 12 hours, flip the cheese, press it together if it is splitting, and continue to dry it for another 12 hours. If using a box, position a fan to blow into the box on low speed for the same amount of time.

4. Remove the parchment paper and place the cheese on a plastic mesh liner or a cooling rack. Continue to dehydrate the cheese for another 12 hours, flip it once more, and dehydrate for 12 more hours. Place a cake pan or a piece of parchment paper beneath the cheese on a lower shelf (or beneath the cooling rack) to catch any coconut oil that might drip off. The time frame for turning the cheese is flexible; you can give or take a few hours to turn it.

5. Wrap the aged cheese in parchment paper and cool in the refrigerator for 6 to 8 hours to firm up. Store the cheese in the parchment for up to 2 weeks. Enjoy the cheese with crackers or fruit, or add it to pasta as you would feta or goat cheese.

Makes 5 ounces

GF, NF, SFO

MAYONNAISE

||||||||||||||||||||||||||||||||||||||||||||||||||||||||

Hunter Noffsinger, of the site PeanutButterandVegan.com, embraced aquafaba a mere few weeks after its discovery and made the emulsification connection right away with her mayonnaise recipe. My version is a simple-to-prepare mayo that makes a delicious spread, dressing, or potato salad. To ensure success, chill your oil in the refrigerator for at least 30 minutes. If making subsequent batches, make sure to cool your blender before proceeding.

> 2 tablespoons Reduced Aquafaba (page 3)
> 1 tablespoon apple cider vinegar
> 1 tablespoon fresh lemon juice
> 1/2 teaspoon nutritional yeast flakes
> 1/2 teaspoon dry mustard
> 1/2 teaspoon sea salt
> 1/8 teaspoon granulated organic sugar
> 1 cup canola or other neutral oil, chilled, divided

1. Add the reduced aquafaba, vinegar, lemon juice, nutritional yeast, mustard, salt, and sugar to a wide-mouth mason jar that will accommodate your immersion blender and blend on low until frothy, about 20 seconds.

2. While blending add the oil in a slow, steady stream. Move the blender stick up and down as needed to allow the blades access to air and create a vortex. Continue blending until all the oil is incorporated and the mayonnaise thickens. The immersion blender yields a thicker mayonnaise than a standard blender.

3. If you make the mayonnaise in a standard blender, add the aquafaba, vinegar, lemon juice, nutritional yeast, mustard, salt, and sugar to a blender jar and blend on low until frothy, about 20 seconds.

4. While blending on low, add 1/4 cup of the oil in a slow, steady stream; this should take about 1 minute and the mixture should be completely emulsified. Increase the speed to medium (or half the power of the blender) and add the remaining 3/4 cup oil in the same manner. Move the base of the machine gently up and down if needed, or move the speed setting of the blender up and down as needed; this will move the air bubble near the base of the jar up and allow the vortex to circulate.

5. Taste and adjust the seasoning with salt and lemon juice. Chill the mayonnaise for 30 minutes to marry the flavors and further thicken. Store in an airtight container in the refrigerator.

||||||||||||||||||||||||||||||||||||||||||||||||||||||||

Makes about 1 1/2 to 1 3/4 cups

GF, NF, SF

TOOM SAUCE

The oil for making this Lebanese sauce needs to be very cold. I put mine in the freezer for about 20 minutes before proceeding with the recipe. Food processors can heat up the emulsion and when that happens, the sauce can break, leaving a puddle of oil and garlic, so chilling the oil well beforehand helps offset the heat from the machine. We love to make quick garlic bread with this sauce, dip pizza into it, or spread it on anything Middle Eastern, such as gyros, shawarmas, or just pita. (See photo on page 21.)

1 tablespoon cold Reduced Aquafaba (page 3)
1/2 cup peeled garlic cloves
3/4 teaspoon sea salt
2 cups very cold canola or other neutral oil, divided
3 tablespoons fresh lemon juice, divided

1. Combine the reduced aquafaba, garlic, and salt in a food processor. Process until the garlic is finely chopped, scraping the sides as needed.

2. With the processor running, add 1/4 cup of the oil in a very thin stream. Add 1 teaspoon of lemon juice. Repeat this process two more times. Stop the machine and scrape the sides and bottom of the bowl.

3. Add the remaining oil in 1/4-cup increments, alternating with 1 teaspoon lemon juice, until all the oil is used. Add the remaining 1 teaspoon lemon juice at the end. Take care that your food processor doesn't overheat as heat can break the emulsion. Transfer the sauce to an airtight container. Store it in the refrigerator for up to 2 weeks.

‖‖‖‖‖‖‖‖‖‖‖‖‖‖‖‖‖‖‖‖‖‖‖‖‖‖‖‖‖‖‖
Makes about 2 1/4 cups

GF, NF, SF

YOGURT

IIIIIIIIIIIIIIIIIIIIIIIIIIIII

Homemade yogurt is the best! I've included two versions, one nut-free and the other soy-free. Use this yogurt in any recipe in the book or just eat it straight from the jar. You can also flavor the plain yogurt with jam or vanilla extract, but make sure to reserve your culture before adding any flavoring. The advantage of using a mother culture is that it does not weaken over subsequent batches, unlike that of a homemade batch cultured with commercial yogurt. Using the below starter dates back to ancient times in India. According to research, it can survive and thrive for years, if not decades.

> **1 quart soymilk (I recommend Westsoy Organic Unsweetened Plain for its purity and high protein content; your milk should have at least 7 grams of protein per cup.)**
> **1 tablespoon granulated organic sugar or maple syrup (if the milk is unsweetened), optional**
> **1/2 cup homemade Mother Culture (see sidebar) or homemade Yogurt (undrained) or 1/4 cup plain unsweetened store-bought nondairy yogurt**

1. Shake the container of soymilk and add it to a large, clean saucepan (or use an Instant Pot if it has the "Yogurt" function). Add the sugar and bring the milk to a boil over medium heat. Boil the milk for 2 to 4 minutes, making sure it does not boil over. If using an Instant Pot, press the "Yogurt" function and then the "Adjust" button until "Boil" appears in the digital window.

2. Remove the mixture from the heat and set it aside to cool to 100 to 110°F, about warm to the touch (use a thermometer to ensure the proper temperature). Do the same if you are using the Instant Pot. Cover it with a lid to prevent a skin from forming.

3. Using a whisk, stir in the mother culture or yogurt—the milk is now "inoculated." Cover the saucepan with wax paper and secure it with a rubber band, or place the Instant Pot insert in the Instant Pot.

4. Transfer the saucepan with the inoculated milk to a warm place. Incubate the yogurt in an environment consistently 110°F for about 6 to 8 hours, or until lightly tangy and semifirm. If using the Instant Pot, push the "Yogurt" function and adjust the time to 8 hours. Place the nozzle in the venting position. Test the yogurt after 6 hours; if it is still too sweet continue to ferment it. The longer it ferments, the thicker and tangier it becomes.

5. Remove 1/2 cup of the undrained yogurt to culture your next batch. Keep in mind that yogurt made from store-bought yogurt will weaken over time.

6. Drain the rest of the yogurt for 2 hours if made with mother culture or yogurt from that generation, or 30 minutes if made with store-bought yogurt, using 8 layers of cheesecloth or a nut-milk bag (preferably made of linen). Place the nut bag over a strainer and the strainer over a bowl. If using the yogurt for cheese, drain it for 24 hours in the refrigerator.

7. Transfer the drained yogurt to a storage container and whisk it for a smooth consistency.

IIIIIIIIIIIIIIIIIIIIIIIIIIIIIIIIIIIIIIIIIIIIIIII

Makes 2 cups + 1/2 cup starter

GF, NF, SFO

Almond-Cashew Yogurt: To make a soy-free yogurt, combine 3 1/2 cups water and 2 cups almond meal in a blender. Blend well, set aside for 5 minutes, and blend again. Strain the milk through a linen or hemp nut-milk bag. Rinse the blender and add the strained almond milk. Add 1 cup raw cashews and blend until perfectly smooth. Use this milk in place of the soymilk to make the yogurt.

How to Develop a Mother Culture

Developing a mother culture is the process of adding wild beneficial bacteria to yogurt without the use of commercial cultures. It is your very first batch of milk that will start to grow the bacterial fermentation. Chile pepper stems contain these wild bacteria and they are used to begin fermenting yogurt. The stems might impart a slight flavor to this original first batch, but once this mother culture is used to ferment subsequent batches of yogurt, the flavor will disappear.

To make the mother culture, cook the milk and inoculate as described on the opposite page, but instead of using yogurt to culture your milk in step 3, use the stems of 10 jalapeño or Fresno chiles and use 3 cups of milk instead of 4; omit the sugar. Cut off the tops of the stems to expose fresh stem and cut the pod just above the seeds, exposing the white pith. Add these stems to the boiled milk after it has cooled to 110°F. Let the yogurt inoculate for 12 to 16 hours, or until thick and tangy. Scrape off the top layer and remove 1/2 cup of this starter yogurt. Discard the rest. Culture your first batch of yogurt using this starter. Remove 1/2 cup of yogurt from any subsequent batches to continue to culture your next batch of yogurt in perpetuity.

Warm Locations for Incubation

- Dehydrator set to 110°F.

- Oven that maintains 110°F with the aid of a pilot light and oven light.

- Wrap the pot in a thick blanket or sleeping bag.

- Place an electric heating pad set to medium between two bath towels on the counter; place the saucepan on the towel and wrap another bath towel over the saucepan to make a warm nest. Transfer the yogurt to 2 (1-quart) jars; place the jars in 3 inches of hot water in an ice chest; reheat the water as needed.

Note: If the temperature is less than 110°F, incubation can take 1 to 2 hours longer. Do not let the yogurt incubate for longer than 11 hours as it can develop a yeasty flavor.

ITALIAN DRESSING

This dressing is reminiscent of the popular casual Italian restaurant salad dressing, only it's better for you. The sunflower seeds give texture of parmesan cheese and a mild eggy flavor. Enjoy it on salad, steamed vegetables, and as a marinade. If it separates slightly, just give it a quick shake.

1/4 cup aquafaba, chilled
1/4 cup canola or other neutral oil, chilled
2 tablespoons Yogurt (page 18) or plain unsweetened store-bought nondairy yogurt
1 to 2 tablespoons white wine vinegar
1 teaspoon fresh lemon juice
1 teaspoon white miso
1 tablespoon nutritional yeast flakes
2 teaspoons granulated organic sugar
1 garlic clove, minced
1/2 teaspoon sea salt
1/4 teaspoon dried parsley or 1 teaspoon minced fresh parsley
1/4 teaspoon dried oregano
1/4 teaspoon dried basil
Pinch red pepper flakes
Ground black pepper, to taste
2 tablespoons finely ground sunflower seeds, optional

1. Add the aquafaba to a wide-mouth pint or quart mason jar. Using an immersion blender that will fit in the jar, blend the aquafaba until frothy, about 20 seconds. While the blender is running, slowly add the oil in a steady stream.

2. When the mixture is homogenous and emulsified, add the yogurt, vinegar, lemon juice, miso, nutritional yeast, sugar, garlic, salt, parsley, oregano, basil, red pepper flakes, and ground black pepper. Blend again. Stir in the sunflower seeds (if using), and chill for 30 minutes before serving.

Makes about 1 cup

GF, NF, SF

From left: Italian Dressing (opposite),
Toom Sauce (page 17), and Caesar Dressing (page 22)

CAESAR DRESSING

IIIIIIIIIIIIIIIIIIIIIIIIIIIIIIIIIIIIIIIIIIIIIIIIIIIIIIIIIIIIIIIIIIIIIIIIIIIIIIIIIIIIIII

Caesar dressing has always been one of my favorites, so, when we became vegan, Robin Robertson's version was a saving grace. Now I make this aquafaba version, a bit unlike Robin's but still very delicious. (See photo on page 21.) Use soy-free yogurt to make this soy-free.

> 1/4 cup aquafaba, chilled
> 1 tablespoon plus 2 teaspoons fresh lemon juice
> 1 tablespoon Yogurt (page 18) or plain unsweetened store-bought nondairy yogurt
> 2 teaspoons white miso
> 1 teaspoon Worcestershire Sauce (page 23) or store-bought vegan Worcestershire sauce
> 2 garlic cloves, minced (about 1 1/2 teaspoons)
> 1 teaspoon capers
> 1/4 teaspoon sea salt
> 1/8 teaspoon ground black pepper
> 2 pinches granulated organic sugar, if yogurt is unsweetened
> 1/2 cup olive oil, chilled
> 1 tablespoon ground sunflower seeds, optional

1. Add the aquafaba, lemon juice, yogurt, miso, Worcestershire Sauce, garlic, capers, salt, black pepper, and sugar (if needed), to the jar of a standard blender. Blend on low until frothy, about 30 seconds. Increase the speed to medium and slowly add the oil in a steady stream.

2. Transfer the mixture to a mason jar and stir in the sunflower seeds, if using. Taste and stir in more lemon juice, if desired. Chill for 30 minutes before serving to meld the flavors and thicken. Store the dressing in an airtight container in the refrigerator for up to 1 week.

IIIIIIIIIIIIIIIIIIIIIIIIIIIIIIIIII

Makes about 1 cup

GF, NF, SFO

WORCESTERSHIRE SAUCE

Homemade vegan Worcestershire sauce is economical and tastes fresher than its store-bought equivalent. In addition to saving money and tasting better, this sauce is easy to make and lasts long in an airtight container in the refrigerator, so there really is no reason not to make a batch.

- 1 cup apple cider vinegar
- 1/2 cup molasses
- 1/2 cup reduced-sodium tamari
- 1/2 cup packed Light Brown Sugar (recipe follows) or store-bought light brown sugar
- 1/2 cup water
- 1/4 cup tamarind concentrate (liquid, not paste)
- 3 teaspoons mustard seeds
- 3 teaspoons sea salt
- 1 1/2 teaspoons ground ginger
- 1 teaspoon black peppercorns
- 1 teaspoon whole cloves
- 2 large garlic cloves, coarsely chopped
- 1 medium onion, coarsely chopped

Combine the vinegar, molasses, tamari, brown sugar, water, tamarind concentrate, mustard seeds, salt, ginger, peppercorns, cloves, garlic, and onion in a medium saucepan. Bring to a boil over high heat, then reduce to a simmer over medium heat, and cook for 10 minutes. Remove from the heat, transfer the mixture to a container, cool it, and refrigerate it overnight or up to 3 days. Strain the liquid, compost or discard the solids, and store the sauce in the refrigerator for up to 3 months.

Makes about 2 1/2 cups

GF, NF, SFO

Soy-Free Option: Omit the tamari. Add 1/2 cup coconut aminos and 1 teaspoon sea salt.

LIGHT BROWN SUGAR

- 2 1/4 cups granulated organic sugar
- 2 tablespoons molasses (preferably blackstrap molasses)

Add the sugar to a food processor and process for 30 seconds. If you process the sugar for 1 minute, it will yield superfine sugar. Add the molasses and process until the mixture is completely homogeneous, scraping the bowl as needed. Store in an airtight container in a cool, dry place to prevent hardening.

Makes about 4 cups

BREAKFAST

Breakfast is traditionally thought of as an array of eggs, eggs, and more eggs. With aquafaba, and a few supporting ingredients, we can make some favorite breakfast dishes vegan. With artillery like fluffy baked doughnuts, crêpes, and crisp waffles, it's time to take breakfast back from the eggs.

Baked Chocolate Cake Doughnuts
and Baked Apple Cider Cake Doughnuts (page28)

BAKED DOUGHNUTS THREE WAYS

These doughnuts bake up beautifully tender. Each batch makes 6 doughnuts, the perfect amount to eat for breakfast with maybe a few left for snacking, but nothing left to go stale. If you have a bigger family and two doughnut pans, double the recipe. Use a piping bag to fill the doughnut tins or just use a large spoon to scoop in the batter. Each recipe is nut-free and can be made soy-free by using soy-free vegan butter.

Baked Chocolate Cake Doughnuts

Chocolate lovers' breakfast dreams do come true. Although not densely chocolatey, this will satisfy your craving, especially if you top it with the glaze.

Doughnuts
1 cup unbleached all-purpose flour
3 tablespoons unsweetened Dutch-process cocoa powder
1 1/4 teaspoons baking powder
1/3 cup granulated organic sugar
1/4 teaspoon salt
5 tablespoons Yogurt (page 18) or store-bought nondairy yogurt
1/4 cup aquafaba
1/4 cup nondairy milk
2 tablespoons nondairy butter, melted
1 teaspoon pure vanilla extract

Chocolate Glaze
2 tablespoons plain unsweetened nondairy milk
1/2 teaspoon nondairy butter
6 tablespoons vegan semisweet chocolate chips
1/4 teaspoon pure vanilla extract

1. Doughnuts: Preheat the oven to 350°F. Spray a 6-well doughnut pan with oil and set aside. Sift the flour, cocoa, and baking powder into a medium bowl. Add the sugar and salt and whisk to combine. Set aside. Combine the yogurt, aquafaba, milk, butter, and vanilla in a medium bowl and whisk well to combine. Add the flour mixture and, using a spatula, fold the ingredients just to combine; lumps are fine and it will be a thick batter.

2. Divide the batter among the 6 doughnut wells using a large spoon or a piping bag; fill each well up to the top and smooth out the batter, if needed. Bake the doughnuts until a toothpick inserted into a doughnut comes out with a few small crumbs attached, 12 to 14 minutes. Cool for 5 minutes before removing them from the pan and placing them on a cooling rack. Let the doughnuts cool before glazing them.

3. Glaze: Heat the milk and butter in a small saucepan until hot but not boiling. Remove the milk mixture from the heat and add the chocolate chips. Set aside for 10 minutes so the chocolate chips can melt. Use a whisk to mix the glaze. Add the vanilla and whisk again. Dip the top of the doughnuts in the glaze and place them on the cooling rack to firm up.

Baked Apple Cider Cake Doughnuts

Apple cider is simply unfiltered apple juice. Use apple cider that isn't spiced, if you can, but if not, then you can omit the spices. The glaze offers the perfect touch of sweetness, but of course, it can be easily skipped.

Doughnuts
3/4 cup apple juice or apple cider
1/3 cup granulated organic sugar
1 1/3 cups plus 1 tablespoon unbleached all-purpose flour
1 1/4 teaspoons baking powder
1 teaspoon pumpkin pie spice, if the cider is not spiced
1/4 teaspoon salt
5 tablespoons Yogurt (page 18) or store-bought nondairy yogurt
1/4 cup aquafaba
2 tablespoons nondairy butter, melted
1 teaspoon pure vanilla extract

Sugar Glaze
6 tablespoons confectioners' sugar
1/4 teaspoon pumpkin spice, if the cider is not spiced
4 teaspoons apple juice or apple cider
Pinch salt

1. Doughnuts: Preheat the oven to 350°F. Spray a 6-well doughnut pan with oil and set aside. Add the apple juice to a small saucepan and bring it to a boil over medium-high heat. Cook the juice until it is reduced to 1/4 cup. Add the sugar, stir to melt, and let the mixture cool slightly.

2. Combine the flour, baking powder, pumpkin pie spice (if using), and salt in a small bowl. Set aside. Combine the reduced apple juice mixture, yogurt, aquafaba, butter, and vanilla in a medium bowl and whisk well to combine. Add the flour mixture and, using a spatula, fold the ingredients just to combine—lumps are fine and it will be a thick batter.

3. Divide the batter among the 6 doughnut wells using a large spoon or a piping bag. Fill each well to the top and smooth out the batter, if needed. Bake until a toothpick inserted into a doughnut comes out with a few small crumbs attached, about 12 minutes. Cool the doughnuts for 5 minutes before removing them from the pan and placing them on a cooling rack. Let the doughnuts cool before glazing them.

4. Glaze: Combine the confectioners' sugar, pumpkin pie spice (if using), apple juice, and salt in a bowl just large enough to dip the doughnuts in. Using a whisk, mix the glaze well. Dip the top of the doughnuts in the icing and place them on the cooling rack to harden.

Baked Blueberry Crumb Doughnuts

This crumb doughnut is beautifully light and tender with a nice bit of crunch from the crumble. You can use a piping bag for the batter, but don't use a tip and cut the opening large enough for the berries to pass through without getting crushed.

Crumb
3 tablespoons unbleached all-purpose flour
3 tablespoons packed Light Brown Sugar (page 23) or store-bought light brown sugar
2 tablespoons rolled oats
1 tablespoon canola or other neutral oil

Doughnuts
3/4 cup plus 3 tablespoons unbleached all-purpose flour
5 tablespoons granulated organic sugar
3/4 teaspoon baking powder
1 teaspoon lemon zest
1/4 teaspoon sea salt
1/8 teaspoon ground nutmeg
5 tablespoons Yogurt (page 18) or store-bought nondairy yogurt
1 tablespoon plain unsweetened nondairy milk
3 tablespoons aquafaba
2 tablespoons nondairy butter, melted
1/2 teaspoon pure vanilla extract
1/3 cup blueberries, partially thawed if frozen

1. **Crumb:** Preheat the oven to 350°F. Spray a 6-well doughnut pan with oil and set aside. Combine the flour, brown sugar, oats, and oil in a small bowl. Mix well and set aside.

2. **Doughnuts:** Combine the flour, sugar, baking powder, zest, salt, and nutmeg in a medium bowl. Set aside. Combine the yogurt, milk, aquafaba, butter, and vanilla in a medium bowl. Whisk well.

3. Add the blueberries to the flour mixture and toss to coat. Add the flour mixture to the yogurt mixture and, using a spatula, fold the ingredients just to combine; the batter will be very thick, which is important for the texture.

4. Divide the batter among the 6 doughnut wells using a large spoon and spread out the batter as much as possible. Sprinkle the doughnuts with the crumb mixture, dividing it equally among the doughnuts. Bake the doughnuts until a toothpick inserted into a doughnut comes out clean, about 22 to 25 minutes. Cool the doughnuts in the pan for 5 minutes before removing them to cool completely on a cooling rack.

CLASSIC WAFFLES

The two most important aspects of a great waffle are crisp exterior and moist and fluffy interior. These deliver big. To make great make-ahead waffles, undercook them by about 1 minute and freeze. When you're ready for them, just toast and enjoy. Serve with vegan butter, maple syrup, or preserves.

2 cups unbleached all-purpose flour
3 tablespoons granulated organic sugar
2 teaspoons baking powder
1 teaspoon sea salt
1 cup nondairy milk
1/2 cup aquafaba
1/4 cup canola or other neutral oil
1 teaspoon pure vanilla extract

1. Combine the flour, sugar, baking powder, and salt in a medium bowl. Whisk or sift to distribute the ingredients equally.

2. Combine the milk, aquafaba, oil, and vanilla in a small bowl and mix well. Add the milk mixture to the flour mixture and whisk gently into a smooth batter. Set the batter aside to hydrate while the waffle iron heats up.

3. Heat the waffle iron according to the manufacturer's instructions, and add the required amount of batter to the hot iron (usually about 1 cup of batter). Cook until the desired doneness is reached and transfer the waffles to a wire rack. The waffles will become crisp in about 30 seconds. Serve hot.

Makes 10 to 12 (3 x 3-inch) waffles

NF, SF

TOASTED OAT WAFFLES

This is a healthier take on the Classic Waffles (page 31), made with plenty of whole-grain oats and apple-sauce in place of the oil. The aquafaba still brings lift and added crispness to the breakfast dish, and the little pieces of oats adds wonderful chew to each bite. Serve with vegan butter, maple syrup, or preserves.

    1 cup plain unsweetened nondairy milk
    1 tablespoon apple cider vinegar
    1 1/4 cups rolled oats
    3/4 cup unbleached all-purpose flour
    3 tablespoons granulated organic sugar
    1 teaspoon sea salt
    1 teaspoon baking powder
    1/2 teaspoon ground cinnamon
    1/4 teaspoon baking soda
    1/4 cup aquafaba
    1/4 cup applesauce

1. Combine the milk and vinegar in a small measuring cup and set aside.

2. Heat a large skillet over medium heat and add the oats. Cook, stirring occasionally, until the oats smell nutty and are light golden, about 6 minutes. Reserve 1/4 cup of the toasted oats and transfer the rest to a food processor. Process the oats into flour; this will take a few minutes in the machine.

3. Add the all-purpose flour, sugar, salt, baking powder, cinnamon, baking soda, and the reserved oats to the food processor. Pulse to combine and break up the added oats. Transfer the mixture to a medium bowl and add the reserved milk mixture, aquafaba, and applesauce. Mix well and set aside to thicken while the waffle iron heats up.

4. Heat the waffle iron according to the manufacturer's instructions, and add the required amount of batter to the hot iron (usually about 1 cup of batter). Cook until the desired doneness is reached and transfer the waffles to a wire rack. Oat waffles will darken sooner than regular waffles. The waffles will become crisp in about 30 seconds. Serve hot.

Makes 10 to 12 (3 x 3-inch) waffles

NF, SF

FLUFFY PANCAKES

||||||||||||||||||||||||||||||||||||||||||||||||||||||||||||||||||||

My youngest daughter is always begging me to make fluffy pancakes, and I have finally reached the fluffy heights that she has been desiring. Use a nonstick griddle, if you have it, or a well-seasoned cast iron skillet. The less time the batter sits, the fluffier your pancakes will be. Serve with maple syrup or preserves. To make soy-free, use soy-free vegan butter.

> 1 cup nondairy milk
> 1 tablespoon apple cider vinegar
> 1 1/4 cups unbleached all-purpose flour
> 1 1/2 teaspoons baking powder
> 1/4 teaspoon baking soda
> 1/4 teaspoon sea salt
> 2 tablespoons aquafaba
> 2 tablespoons granulated organic sugar, divided
> 2 tablespoons canola or other neutral oil
> 1 teaspoon pure vanilla extract
> Butter (page 10) or store-bought nondairy butter, as needed

1. Combine the milk and vinegar in a small measuring cup and set aside to thicken for 10 minutes.

2. Combine the flour, baking powder, baking soda, and salt in a large bowl. Mix well and set aside.

3. Add the aquafaba to a small bowl and, using a small whisk, beat well for 1 minute until white and frothy. Add 1 tablespoon of the sugar and whip for another minute. Add the remaining 1 tablespoon sugar and whip for another minute. Set aside.

4. Heat a griddle or large skillet over medium-low heat. Add the milk mixture, oil, vanilla, and aquafaba mixture to the flour mixture. Stir to mix the ingredients. Do not overmix; there should still be lumps and a few flour spots.

5. Lightly butter the skillet and add portions of the batter in 1/3-cup measurements. Cook until the pancakes are light golden brown on the bottom and until the edges of the top of the pancakes are drying out, about 1 minute. Flip the pancakes and continue to cook until golden brown on the other side, about another minute. Serve hot.

||||||||||||||||||||||||||||||||||||
Makes 8 pancakes

NF, SFO

LEMON POPPY SEED MUFFINS

My eldest daughter has always loved lemon poppy seed muffins and was thrilled when I was able to make this tender and beautiful vegan version. The lemon is subtle if you use only the zest, so if you love it with more of a lemon punch, add the optional extract.

> 2 2/3 cups unbleached all-purpose flour
> 2 tablespoons poppy seeds
> 2 3/4 teaspoons baking powder
> 1/2 teaspoon sea salt
> 1/3 cup aquafaba
> 1/3 cup canola or other neutral oil
> 3/4 cup plus 2 tablespoons granulated organic sugar
> 1 cup nondairy milk
> 1 1/2 teaspoons pure vanilla extract
> 3/4 teaspoon pure lemon extract, optional
> 1 tablespoon lemon zest (from approximately 2 lemons)
> 3 tablespoons coarse or raw sugar

1. Preheat the oven to 375°F. Line a 12-well regular-size muffin tin with paper cups or spray the wells with oil. Set the tin aside.

2. Combine the flour, poppy seeds, baking powder, and salt in a medium bowl. Mix well and set aside.

3. Place a separate medium bowl on a folded kitchen towel. Add the aquafaba and, using a large whisk, whisk it until it is frothy, about 1 minute. Add the oil slowly while whisking to emulsify. Add the sugar in the same way. Add the milk, vanilla, lemon extract (if using), and zest and whisk well.

4. Add the flour mixture to the milk mixture and, using a wooden spoon, mix the batter until almost no more flour is visible. Lumps are fine; do not overmix.

5. Fill the wells about three-quarters full with the batter and sprinkle the coarse sugar on top. Bake the muffins until a toothpick inserted into the muffin in the middle well comes out clean, 17 to 20 minutes.

6. Cool the muffins on a cooling rack for 15 minutes before removing them from the tin. Cool the muffins completely before storing in airtight containers, where they will keep for a few days.

Makes 12 muffins

NF, SF

FRENCH TOAST

||||||||||||||||||||||||||||||||||||||||||||||||||||

The best French toast is one that is custardy on the inside and crispy on the outside. Eggs typically provide the custardy texture, but cashews and aquafaba provide the needed structure in this version. Use Challah (page 66) that is at least a few days old, or use French or Italian bread that is at least a day old. Using fresh bread will result in soggy, not custardy, French toast. Serve with maple syrup or preserves. To make soy-free, use soy-free vegan butter.

> **3/4 cup nondairy milk**
> **1/4 cup plus 2 tablespoons raw cashew pieces**
> **1/2 cup aquafaba**
> **1 tablespoon maple syrup**
> **Pinch salt**
> **8 to 12 (3/4-inch thick) bread slices, depending on the size of the bread**
> **Butter (page 10) or store-bought nondairy butter, as needed**

1. Combine the milk, cashews, aquafaba, syrup, and salt in a blender. Blend until smooth. If you are using a regular blender, allow the nuts to soak for 10 minutes and blend again until the mixture is smooth. Transfer the mixture to a shallow pan.

2. Heat a large skillet over medium heat and preheat the oven to 400°F. Add 4 pieces of the bread to the custard and allow the bread to soak for up to 1 minute on each side, depending on how dry the bread is. Melt 1 teaspoon butter in the skillet and add the soaked bread slices. Cook the bread for 2 minutes, flip, and cook the other side until golden brown, 1 to 2 minutes. Repeat this process with the remaining 4 slices of bread.

3. Transfer the French toast to the rack of the oven and bake for 5 to 8 minutes. Remove it from the oven and set aside for 30 seconds; the bread will become crisp in that time. Serve hot.

|||||||||||||||||||||||||||||
Makes 4 servings

SFO

FRITTATA

Frittata is the Italian version of a baked omelet, but with the addition of meats, cheeses, and vegetables. With a delicate crust and creamy inside, frittatas are well-loved egg-based dishes, but in this vegan version, the tofu acts as the protein base that aquafaba is lacking. This is not just a glorified tofu scramble. For best results, use an oven-safe nonstick pan. If you have a scale, start with 200 grams of tofu.

- 1 1/3 cups well-crumbled firm tofu, lightly drained and loosely packed
- 3 tablespoons unbleached all-purpose flour
- 1 tablespoon plus 1 teaspoon packed chickpea flour
- 1 tablespoon nutritional yeast flakes
- 1 1/2 teaspoons psyllium husk powder
- 1/4 teaspoon turmeric
- 1/4 teaspoon sea salt, plus more to taste
- 1/2 cup plus 2 tablespoons aquafaba
- 6 tablespoons water
- 1 1/2 tablespoons canola or other neutral oil
- 1 tablespoon white miso
- 1 tablespoon Butter (page 10) or store-bought nondairy butter
- 1/2 teaspoon toasted sesame seed oil
- 1 small red bell pepper, coarsely chopped
- 4 scallions, finely chopped
- 1 medium yellow squash, coarsely chopped
- Ground black pepper, to taste
- 1/4 cup chopped fresh basil or 2 tablespoons chopped fresh parsley
- Black salt, optional

1. Preheat the oven to 325°F. Combine the tofu, all-purpose flour, chickpea flour, nutritional yeast, psyllium husk powder, turmeric, salt, aquafaba, water, canola oil, and miso in a blender. Blend until very smooth and immediately transfer the mixture to a large bowl. Set aside for 10 minutes to thicken.

2. Heat the butter and sesame oil in a 9-inch, oven-safe skillet over medium heat. Add the bell pepper and cook until softened, about 3 minutes. Add the scallions and squash, season with salt and black pepper, and continue to cook until the squash is lightly golden, about 5 more minutes. Scatter the basil over the vegetables and pour the batter over the vegetable mixture. Move the vegetables around lightly to allow the batter to disperse evenly. Cook for 2 minutes and transfer the skillet to the oven. Bake for 50 to 60 minutes. Remove from the oven and allow it to set up for 10 minutes. Serve sprinkled with black salt (if using).

Makes 2 servings

NF, SFO

Soy-Free Option: Use soy-free vegan butter and substitute 3/4 cup raw cashew pieces (see Nuts, blending, page 166) for the tofu.

TAMAGOYAKI ROLLED OMELET

The topping is important for the texture of this omelet. It is also important to measure the chickpea flour properly; stir the flour and, using a large spoon, scoop the flour into the measuring cup. Use the back of a knife to level off the flour. This omelet is very much like the traditional Japanese omelet that is rolled and packed in bento boxes for lunch. If you have a scale, use 56 grams of chickpea flour.

> 6 tablespoons aquafaba
> 1/8 teaspoon cream of tartar
> 4 teaspoons canola or other neutral oil, divided
> 2 scallions, minced
> 1 small Fresno chile, seeded and minced
> 1 cup plain unsweetened nondairy milk
> 1/4 cup Yogurt (page 18) or plain unsweetened store-bought nondairy yogurt
> 1/2 cup plus 1 tablespoon chickpea flour
> 1 tablespoon nutritional yeast flakes
> 3/4 teaspoon sea salt
> 2 pinches turmeric
> Ground black pepper, to taste
> 1/4 teaspoon black salt, optional (but decrease the sea salt by the same amount)

1. Add the aquafaba and cream of tartar to the bowl of a stand mixer. Using a whisk, whip the aquafaba until foamy, about 30 seconds. Add a balloon whip attachment and whip for 5 minutes on medium-low speed. Increase the speed to medium-high and continue to whip for another 4 to 5 minutes, or until the meringue makes firm peaks (page 5).

2. Heat 2 teaspoons of the oil over medium heat in a small skillet or saucepan and add the scallions and chile. Cook until softened, about 3 minutes. Season with salt and black pepper. Set aside.

3. Add the milk, yogurt, chickpea flour, nutritional yeast, salt, turmeric, black pepper, and the remaining 2 teaspoons oil to a blender. Blend until very smooth. Transfer this mixture to a medium saucepan. Cook over medium heat until the mixture comes to a simmer, then reduce the heat to medium-low and cook for 8 to 10 minutes, whisking constantly to avoid lumps. This is important to ensure that the flour is cooked all the way through. Lower the heat to low (if the mixture begins to cool it will firm up and be difficult to work with).

4. Add the black salt (if using) to the flour mixture and whisk well. Add a whisk full of foam and fold to combine using the whisk. Repeat until up to two-thirds of the foam is used; discard the rest of the foam. Continue to fold until there is no white foam evident in the mixture. The foam will deflate some but not completely. The amount of foam you add will determine how light the final omelet will be.

5. Immediately transfer the mixture to a 16 x 11-inch silicone mat or the back of an oiled baking sheet and, using an offset spatula, spread the omelet mixture almost to the edges. Sprinkle the omelet evenly with the reserved scallions and chile. Add black salt to taste (if using), and let the omelet cool completely.

6. Loosen a short edge of the omelet and, using the mat to help you roll and a spatula to loosen any stuck portions, roll up the omelet as tightly as you can. Cut into 2-inch pieces and chill them in the refrigerator for 15 minutes to firm up.

‖‖‖‖‖‖‖‖‖‖‖‖‖‖‖‖‖‖‖‖‖‖‖‖‖‖
Makes 4 servings

GF, NF, SF

Variation: For the topping, cook 1 teaspoon mustard seeds, 1 teaspoon cumin seeds, and a few pinches of asafoetida, (a common Indian spice that has both garlic and onion flavors) in the oil until the seeds sputter. Carefully add 2 tablespoons chopped fresh cilantro leaves (the oil will sputter), and cook for another few seconds until the cilantro crisps a bit.

MATZO BREI

||||||||||||||||||||||||||||||||||||||||||||||

This take on the traditional Jewish matzo brei is just as great as the original. The tofu in this case is just a base for the rest of the egg-like mixture, and it is miles away from a tofu scramble. The matzos give the tofu and aquafaba the needed starch to make it fluffy and light. If you have a scale, use 135 grams of tofu.

1 cup well-crumbled firm tofu, lightly drained and loosely packed
1 tablespoon packed chickpea flour
2 teaspoons nutritional yeast flakes
1 teaspoon psyllium husk powder
1/4 teaspoon sea salt, plus more to taste
1/8 teaspoon turmeric
7 tablespoons aquafaba
1/4 cup water
1 tablespoon canola or other neutral oil
3 sheets matzos
1 tablespoon Butter (page 10) or store-bought nondairy butter
Ground black pepper, to taste

1. Combine the tofu, chickpea flour, nutritional yeast, psyllium husk powder, salt, turmeric, aquafaba, water, and oil in a blender. Blend until very smooth and immediately transfer to a large bowl. Set aside for 10 minutes to thicken. Break the matzos into bite-size pieces into a medium bowl. Add enough water to cover and soak the matzos for 30 seconds. Drain well, gently squeezing out excess moisture.

2. Heat the butter in a medium skillet over medium-low heat. Add the drained matzos, arranging them in the skillet and pour the tofu batter over the matzos. Using a spatula, move the batter around so that it is evenly spread. Cook for 4 minutes, moving the batter around every minute or so. Flip portions of the mixture when it is set on the bottom and repeat as desired until the batter is mostly set and the matzo is golden, about 3 more minutes.

3. Season the matzo brei with salt and black pepper. Remove it from the heat and allow it to set and firm up for 30 seconds before serving.

||||||||||||||||||||||||||||||||||||||||||||||||||||||||||||||||||||||||||||||||
Makes 4 servings as a side dish or 2 servings as a main dish

NF

CRÊPES

These paper-thin pancakes are quite similar to the Indian dosa, Mexican tortilla, or African injera. Crêpes can be savory, but they are more typically served with fresh fruit, whipped toppings, ganache, or preserves. This recipe easily lends itself to either savory or sweet. Be prepared to ruin your first crêpe of the batch, as it is a traditional happenstance.

> 1 1/4 cups plain unsweetened nondairy milk
> 6 tablespoons aquafaba
> 2 tablespoons canola or other neutral oil
> 1 cup unbleached all-purpose flour
> Butter (page 10) or store-bought nondairy butter, as needed

1. Combine the milk, aquafaba, oil, and flour in a blender. Blend for 10 seconds to avoid overmixing. Set the batter aside for 30 minutes.

2. Heat a 9- or 10-inch crêpe pan or nonstick pan over medium heat. Melt 1/4 teaspoon butter in the pan and ladle in about 1/4 cup of the batter. Swirl and tilt the pan to evenly coat the bottom of the skillet. Cook the crêpe until light golden brown on the bottom, about 2 minutes. Flip the crêpe and cook for another 15 seconds. Chances are good that the first crêpe will be a flop, so discard it and continue to cook the rest of the batter.

3. Stack the crêpes as they are cooked. Fill them as desired and serve.

Makes 8 crêpes

NF, SF

LUNCH AND DINNER

There are plenty of egg-based dishes that are for other meals besides breakfast. Rich and creamy quiches and burgers come to mind, in which eggs are used for everything from leavening to offering moisture and binding. This chapter has all kinds of offerings for the rest of the day, from eggroll wrappers, which can be used to make appetizers or crispy toppings for soups and salads, to breads and rolls.

LATKES

These latkes are perfectly crisp on the outside and melt-in-your-mouth on the inside. The added potato starch increases their crispiness, but it is not essential. Some russet potatoes tend to be on the drier side, but to be safe, place them in a lint-free kitchen towel, fold up the edges and give them a good wring to remove excess water. Serve this the traditional way, with nondairy sour cream and applesauce.

> 2 pounds russet potatoes
> 1/2 medium onion
> 1/4 cup aquafaba
> 1/4 cup potato starch, optional
> 2 tablespoons minced fresh parsley, optional
> 1/2 teaspoon sea salt
> 1/2 teaspoon baking powder
> 1/4 teaspoon ground black pepper
> High-heat oil, for frying, such as canola or peanut

1. Peel the potatoes and shred them using either a food processor with the shredding blade or a box grater. Place them on a kitchen towel, fold up the edges, twist the towel around the potatoes, and squeeze out all the water that you can. Place the potatoes in a large bowl. Shred the onion and add it to the potatoes. Add the aquafaba, starch, parsley (if using), salt, baking powder, and black pepper. Mix very well.

2. Heat about 1/2 inch of oil in a large skillet over medium heat. Add two or three kernels of popping corn and heat the oil until the corn pops; this is an indicator that your oil is hot enough. Remove and discard the popped corn.

3. Using a 1/4-cup measuring cup, place 3 to 4 portions of the potato mixture in the hot oil and cook them until golden brown, about 2 minutes. Do not press down on the latkes. Flip the latkes and continue to cook another 2 minutes. Drain them on paper towels and serve as soon as possible. Make sure to give the potatoes a stir before measuring, and do not crowd the skillet or your latkes will not be crispy.

Makes 14 to 16 latkes

GF, NF, SF

EGGROLL WRAPPERS

This is a wonderfully easy dough to work with, and you will be pleased at how well it rolls and reacts for you. You can even make these into wontons for soup, simmering them until cooked. They fry up like egg-based rolls and strips and stay crisp, as long as your filling is well drained and cooled.

> 2 cups unbleached all-purpose flour
> 1 teaspoon sea salt
> 1 teaspoon psyllium husk powder
> 6 tablespoons aquafaba, cold
> 5 1/2 to 6 tablespoons ice-cold water
> Cornstarch or arrowroot starch, for rolling and dusting

1. Combine the flour, salt, and psyllium husk powder in a medium bowl. Add the aquafaba and 5 tablespoons water. Mix together and add more water as needed, up to 1 more tablespoon to achieve a soft dough. Knead the dough for 3 to 5 minutes. Wrap the dough in wax paper or put it into an airtight container and refrigerate it for at least 30 minutes (but 1 hour is better).

2. Divide the dough in two. Dust your work surface with a few tablespoons of cornstarch and roll one of the dough halves into a large rectangle (do the best that you can). The dough should be about 1/16-inch thick. Cut the rectangle into 6- x 6-inch squares, dust with more cornstarch, and stack until needed. Make sure to keep the stack covered to prevent the wrappers from drying out.

3. Alternatively, cut the dough into 3- x 3-inch squares for wonton wrappers or 1- x 3-inch strips for fried wonton strips.

4. To ensure that your fried rolls are crisp, make sure that your filling is well drained and cool; otherwise, you will yield soggy eggrolls.

Makes 28 to 30 (4- x 4-inch) wrappers

NF, SF

GALUSHKA

Galushka is the Hungarian version of the everyday egg-based pasta that is popular among most European cultures. It's more commonly known as spätzle, nokedli, chnöpfli, or knöpfle. This is a very quickly made dumpling that is toothsome yet still tender and very versatile. A few tablespoons of any minced fresh herbs can be added, as well as minced roasted garlic or minced caramelized onions. Serve this pasta with Chickpea Gulyás (page 150). (See photo on page 151.)

> 1 cup semolina flour
> 1/2 cup unbleached all-purpose flour
> 1 teaspoon psyllium husk powder
> 1 1/2 teaspoons sea salt
> 1/2 cup aquafaba
> 6 tablespoons plain unsweetened nondairy milk
> 1/4 cup canola or other neutral oil

1. Combine the semolina flour, all-purpose flour, psyllium husk powder, and salt in a medium bowl. Add the aquafaba, milk, and oil and mix only until combined. Set the dough aside to firm up while you heat the water.

2. Bring a medium saucepan of water to boil. Transfer the dough to a damp cutting board; it will be very loose and sticky. If necessary, flatten it to a 1/2-inch thickness. Using a paring knife or spoon, cut off pieces of the dough and push them (or, if using a spoon, pull them) into the boiling water. The pieces of dough can be small or large, but keep them uniform in size for even cooking. Dip your knife or spoon into the water to prevent the dough from sticking to it; do this after each piece, while giving the water a quick stir to move the dumplings around. Cook the galushka until firm, about 3 to 4 minutes. They will begin to float to the top of the water. Drain the galushka well and serve them immediately or toss them with a teaspoon of oil to prevent them from sticking together.

Makes 4 to 6 servings as a side dish

NF, SF

CHILE RELLENO QUICHE

Traditional chiles relleno are made with roasted poblano chiles stuffed with cheese, battered with eggs, and deep-fried. This creamy, delicious quiche offers all the flavors of a really excellent chile relleno. Most poblanos are relatively mild, but nothing is for sure these days where the heat of chiles is concerned. If you do not care for any heat, substitute 2 large green bell peppers for the poblanos. On the other hand, if you like more heat, add a few roasted jalapeños to the mix. If you have a scale, use 45 grams of oat flour.

>   3/4 cup raw cashew pieces
>   3/4 cup Yogurt (page 18) or plain unsweetened store-bought nondairy yogurt
>   4 medium poblano chiles
>   3/4 cup aquafaba
>   1/4 teaspoon cream of tartar
>   2 tablespoons refined coconut oil, just melted and at room temperature
>   1/2 cup plus 1 tablespoon oat flour
>   5 teaspoons nutritional yeast flakes
>   1 teaspoon sea salt
>   1/4 teaspoon turmeric
>   1/4 teaspoon garlic powder
>   Ground black pepper, to taste
>   1 (9-inch) Traditional Pie Crust (page 92), par-baked for 12 minutes, or store-bought
>   vegan pie crust

1. Preheat the oven to 325°F. Combine the cashews and yogurt in a blender and blend until smooth, scraping the sides as needed. If using a standard blender, allow the nuts to hydrate for 10 minutes and blend again until smooth. Set aside.

2. Roast the poblanos directly over the flame of your burner or roast them in a cast iron pan. Cook until blackened and charred all over. Transfer the poblanos to a bowl, cover the bowl with a plate, and set aside to steam for 15 minutes. Peel the poblanos (do not wash them) and remove the stems and seeds. Chop the poblanos into 1/2-inch cubes and set aside. You should have about 1 1/2 cups chopped chiles.

3. Add the aquafaba and cream of tartar to the bowl of a stand mixer. Using a whisk, vigorously whip the aquafaba for 10 seconds. Using the balloon whip attachment, whip the aquafaba on medium power for 5 minutes. Increase the speed to medium-high and continue to whip for 11 to 13 minutes, or until it forms stiff peaks (page 5). Add the oil to the meringue in a very slow, steady stream, pouring it down the side of the bowl. This should take about 1 minute.

4. Combine the oat flour, nutritional yeast, salt, turmeric, garlic powder, and black pepper. Mix well. Add the nut mixture and mix well with a whisk. Transfer about one-half of the meringue to the oat mixture and fold with a spatula to incorporate. Transfer the rest of the meringue to the tempered batter and fold until the batter is well mixed and the meringue is deflated, adding the chopped poblanos toward the end of the folding process.

5. Pour the batter into the par-baked pie crust and bake for 40 minutes. Increase the heat to 425°F and continue to bake until the top is golden, about 5 minutes. Chill the quiche overnight in the refrigerator to firm up.

‖‖‖‖‖‖‖‖‖‖‖‖‖‖‖‖‖‖‖‖‖‖‖‖‖‖‖‖‖‖‖‖

Makes 1 (9-inch) quiche

GF, NFO, SF

Nut-Free Option: Substitute 1 cup firm tofu, lightly drained and mashed, for the nuts.

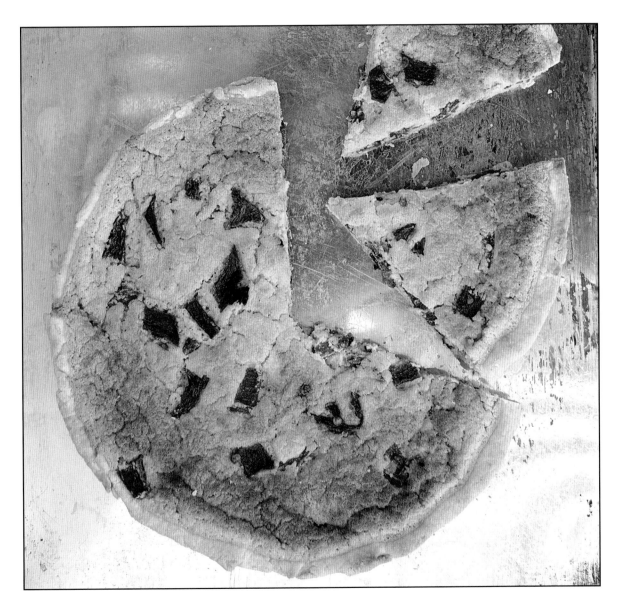

SUN-DRIED TOMATO AND ARTICHOKE QUICHE

Creamy and rich, this quiche is also versatile. If you don't care for sun-dried tomatoes or artichokes, swap them out for something comparable, but make sure there is no added moisture like there would be with using fresh tomatoes or raw greens, since that could upset the delicate balance of the batter. This makes a great lunch or dinner meal with an added side salad. If you have a scale, use 45 grams of oat flour.

3/4 cup raw cashew pieces
3/4 cup plain unsweetened nondairy milk
1 teaspoon vegan lactic acid or lemon juice
3/4 cup aquafaba
1/4 teaspoon cream of tartar
2 tablespoons refined coconut oil, just melted and at room temperature
1 tablespoon olive oil
1 (15-ounce) can artichokes, drained, rinsed, and coarsely chopped
4 garlic cloves, minced

4 sun-dried tomato halves (about 1/4 cup), rehydrated in hot water, drained, and minced
1/2 cup plus 1 tablespoon oat flour
5 teaspoons nutritional yeast flakes
1 teaspoon sea salt
1/4 teaspoon turmeric
Ground black pepper, to taste
1 (9-inch) Traditional Pie Crust (page 92), par-baked for 12 minutes, or store-bought vegan pie crust

1. Preheat the oven to 325°F. Combine the cashews, milk, and lactic acid in a blender and blend until smooth, scraping the sides as needed. If using a standard blender, allow the nuts to hydrate for 10 minutes and blend again until smooth. Set aside.

2. Add the aquafaba and cream of tartar to the bowl of a stand mixer. Using a whisk, vigorously whip the aquafaba for 10 seconds. Using the balloon whip attachment, whip the aquafaba on medium-low power for 5 minutes. Increase the speed to medium-high and continue to whip for 11 to 13 minutes, or until it forms stiff peaks (page 5). Add the coconut oil to the meringue in a very slow, steady stream, pouring it down the side of the bowl. This should take about 1 minute.

3. Heat the olive oil in a medium skillet over medium heat. Add the artichokes and cook until golden, about 8 minutes. Add the garlic and tomatoes and cook for another minute. Set aside.

4. Combine the oat flour, nutritional yeast, salt, turmeric, and black pepper. Mix well. Add the nut mixture and mix well with a whisk. Transfer about one-half of the meringue to the oat mixture and fold with a spatula to incorporate. Transfer the rest of the meringue to the tempered batter and fold until the batter is well mixed and the meringue is deflated, adding the artichoke mixture toward the end of the folding process.

5. Pour the batter into a par-baked pie crust and bake for 40 minutes, tenting the quiche with foil if it is darkening too quickly. If the quiche is not golden brown, increase the heat to 425°F and continue to bake until the top is golden, about 5 minutes. Chill the quiche completely before serving.

Makes 1 (9-inch) quiche

GF, NFO, SF

Nut-Free Option: Substitute 1 cup firm tofu, mashed and lightly drained, for the nuts.

PORTOBELLO SCHNITZEL

Schnitzel's appeal is the batter. Egg batters create a different crispiness, and the breading's texture is distinctive in the sense that it clings to the ingredients better and renders a crispy, crunchy crust. This aquafaba version takes me back to my childhood, but in a much better way.

> 1/2 cup unbleached all-purpose flour
> 2/3 cup dried breadcrumbs
> 1/2 cup aquafaba
> 1 tablespoon canola or other neutral oil, plus more for frying
> 3/4 teaspoon psyllium husk powder
> 1/2 teaspoon sea salt
> 1/2 teaspoon nutritional yeast flakes
> 1/2 teaspoon paprika
> 1/2 teaspoon granulated garlic
> 6 small to medium portobello mushrooms (the thinner the better)
> Lemon wedges, for garnishing

1. Add the flour to a shallow container and set aside. Add the breadcrumbs to a separate shallow container and set aside. Add the aquafaba, 1 tablespoon of the oil, psyllium husk powder, salt, nutritional yeast, paprika, and granulated garlic to a third shallow container and mix well with a whisk.

2. Clean the mushrooms by wiping them with a cloth, removing the stems, and scraping out the gills with a spoon. Dip a mushroom into the flour, coating well and shaking off excess flour, then into the aquafaba mixture, again coating well and dripping off excess wash. Finally, coat well with the breadcrumbs. Repeat this process with all the mushrooms.

3. Heat 1/2 inch of oil in a large cast iron skillet until a popcorn kernel added to the oil pops, indicating the oil is hot. Add the battered mushrooms and cook until golden brown, about 1 minute per side. Drain the mushrooms on paper towels. Serve the portobello schnitzel with slices of lemon wedges.

Makes 4 to 6 servings

NF, SF

Variation: Use firm tofu, drained and pressed for 1 hour and cut into 1/4-inch thick slabs. Or use seitan that has been cut into 1/4-inch thick slices.

Baked Schnitzel: Batter the mushrooms, tofu, or seitan, as instructed above. Spray them with oil. Bake them until crisp in a preheated 375°F oven for 30 minutes, flipping after 15 minutes.

FASÍRT HUNGARIAN BURGERS

Fasírt, the Hungarian version of a hamburger, is always dredged in fine breadcrumbs and deep-fried. I've opted to pan-fry these vegan burgers, but thanks to the aquafaba, they are just as moist and tender while still being firm. Hungarians don't serve these burgers as we do; in fact, they serve them with a creamy stew, like Green Bean Főzelék or Zucchini Főzelék, which are variations on the Chickpea and Zucchini Főzelék (page 143).

1 teaspoon olive oil
1 cup cooked chickpeas, lightly mashed
1/2 small head cauliflower (about 9 ounces), finely chopped
1/2 medium onion, coarsely chopped
4 garlic cloves, minced
1/4 cup coarsely chopped fresh parsley
1/2 teaspoon dried sage
1/2 teaspoon dried thyme
Vegetable broth, as needed for deglazing
1/2 cup unbleached all-purpose flour
1/4 cup raw unsalted pepitas
1 tablespoon nutritional yeast flakes
1 teaspoon Hungarian paprika

3 tablespoons tapioca starch
3 tablespoons brown rice flour
1 teaspoon psyllium husk powder
Ground black pepper, to taste
1 teaspoon sea salt
1/4 cup plus 1 tablespoon aquafaba
1/8 teaspoon cream of tartar
1 tablespoon ketchup
1 tablespoon Worcestershire Sauce (page 23) or store-bought vegan Worcestershire sauce
1/2 cup dry breadcrumbs
High-heat oil, for pan-frying

1. Heat the oil in a large skillet over medium heat. Add the chickpeas, cauliflower, onion, garlic, parsley, sage, and thyme. Cover and cook, stirring occasionally, until the cauliflower is almost tender, 8 to 13 minutes. Deglaze with splashes of broth to prevent sticking, as needed.

2. Add the all-purpose flour, pepitas, nutritional yeast, and paprika. Stir well and cook until the flour is well incorporated, about 3 minutes. Transfer the mixture to a food processor, add the tapioca starch, brown rice flour, psyllium husk powder, black pepper, and salt and pulse 8 to 10 times. The mixture should not be a purée. Transfer the mixture to a large bowl.

3. Make the meringue by adding the aquafaba and cream of tartar to the bowl of a stand mixer. Using a whisk, vigorously whip the aquafaba for 10 seconds. Using the balloon whip attachment, whip the aquafaba on medium-low speed for 5 minutes. Increase the speed to medium-high and continue to whip until the meringue forms firm peaks (page 5), 4 to 5 more minutes.

4. Add the ketchup, Worcestershire sauce, and whipped aquafaba to the chickpea mixture. Fold the mixture together until well mixed. Form the mixture into 10 patties or 20 mini burgers and dredge in the breadcrumbs.

5. Heat about 1/4 inch of oil in a large skillet and fry the burgers until golden brown, about 2 minutes per side. Drain the burgers on paper towels and serve.

|||||||||||||||||||||||||||||||||||||||||||||||||||||||||||||||||||

Makes 10 burgers or 20 mini burgers

GFO, NF, SF

Gluten-Free Option: Substitute 1/2 cup oat flour for the all-purpose flour. Use gluten-free breadcrumbs.

LEVANTINE KEBABS

Cuisine of the Levant, or Eastern Mediterranean, makes popular use of skewers of spiced ground meat. In this recipe, I use cracked freekeh, chickpeas, gluten, and meringue to create stick-to-your-ribs kebabs. The kebabs are crisp on the outside and moist and tender on the inside. You can also par-bake these and cool them for later grilling outdoors.

> **2 teaspoons ground cumin**
> **2 teaspoons ground sumac**
> **1/2 to 1 teaspoon red pepper flakes**
> **1 cup vegetable broth**
> **1/3 cup cracked freekeh**
> **4 tablespoons olive oil, divided**
> **1/4 cup plus 2 tablespoons aquafaba, divided**
> **2 cups cooked chickpeas**
> **1 cup fresh parsley leaves, loosely packed**
> **3 garlic cloves, finely chopped**
> **1 teaspoon sea salt, divided**
> **3/4 cup vital wheat gluten flour, stirred before measuring**
> **12 skewers**
> **Pita bread and Toom Sauce (page 17), for serving**
> **Slices of tomato and red onion, for serving**

1. Preheat the oven to 400°F. Make the seasoning mix by combining the cumin, sumac, and red pepper flakes. Set aside. Combine the broth, freekeh, and 1 tablespoon of the olive oil in a small saucepan. Bring the broth mixture to a boil over medium-high heat, reduce to a simmer over medium heat, and cook until the freekeh is tender, 10 to 20 minutes, depending on the size of the freekeh; add more broth if needed. Set the freekeh aside to cool for 5 minutes. Drain well using a fine-mesh strainer.

2. Add 1/4 cup of the aquafaba to the bowl of a stand mixer and whip on medium-high until firm peaks (page 5) form, about 8 to 10 minutes.

3. Add the chickpeas, parsley, garlic, 3/4 teaspoon of the salt, and 2 teaspoons of the spice mixture to the a food processor. Process until the chickpeas are finely ground. Transfer the chickpea mixture to a large bowl and stir in the freekeh and gluten flour. Add the whipped aquafaba and fold to combine.

4. Combine the remaining spice mixture with the remaining 3 tablespoons olive oil, 2 tablespoons aquafaba, and 1/4 teaspoon salt in a small bowl; mix well to form a paste and set aside. Divide the freekeh mixture into 12 equal portions and form each portion around a skewer, about 1-inch wide and 1-inch thick oblong shapes, squeezing the mixture to compress it well. This is easiest to do by placing the mixture in the palm of your hand, placing a skewer in the middle of the mixture, and forming the mixture around the skewer; use the palms of your hands to form and compress the mixture all along the skewer. The kebabs can double in size as they bake.

5. Place each kebab on a lightly oiled baking sheet and baste them with the spice paste. Bake the kebabs for 15 minutes, flip, baste with the spice paste, and continue to bake until brown and crisp on the outside, another 20 minutes. Remove the kebabs from the oven and set them aside to firm up for 5 minutes. Serve the kebabs with pita, toom sauce, and slices of tomato and onion.

|||||||||||||||||||||||||||||||||||||||||||||||||

Makes 12 to 13 kebabs

NF, SF

ITALIAN MEATBALLS

You can make these delicious fluffy meatballs ahead of time and bake them as needed, but par-bake them for 30 minutes; otherwise, they will dry out. We love these with spaghetti and tomato sauce or on subs with tomato sauce and vegan cheese.

  4 tablespoons olive oil, divided
  1 cup cooked chickpeas, lightly mashed
  1/2 small head cauliflower (about 9 ounces), sliced paper thin
  1/2 medium onion, sliced paper thin
  8 garlic cloves, minced
  1 teaspoon dried oregano
  1 teaspoon dried basil
  1 teaspoon fennel seeds
  1/8 to 1/2 teaspoon red pepper flakes
  Vegetable broth, as needed for deglazing
  1/2 cup unbleached all-purpose flour
  1/4 cup raw unsalted pepitas, coarsely chopped
  3 tablespoons tapioca starch
  3 tablespoons brown rice flour
  1 teaspoon psyllium husk powder
  Ground black pepper, to taste
  1 teaspoon sea salt
  1 tablespoon ketchup
  1 tablespoon white miso or chickpea miso
  1 tablespoon Worcestershire Sauce (page 23) or store-bought vegan Worcestershire sauce
  1/2 cup panko breadcrumbs
  1/4 cup plus 1 tablespoon aquafaba, divided
  1/8 teaspoon cream of tartar

1. Heat 1 teaspoon of the olive oil in a large skillet over medium heat. Add the chickpeas, cauliflower, onion, garlic, oregano, basil, fennel, and red pepper flakes. Cover and cook, stirring occasionally, until the cauliflower and chickpeas turn dark golden brown, about 14 minutes. Deglaze with splashes of broth to prevent burning, as needed.

2. Add the all-purpose flour and pepitas. Stir well and cook until the flour smells nutty and is turning darker, about 3 minutes. Transfer the mixture to a food processor, add the tapioca starch, brown rice flour, psyllium husk powder, black pepper, and salt and pulse 7 to 8 times. Transfer the coarse mixture to a large bowl. Combine the ketchup, miso, and Worcestershire Sauce in a small bowl and mix until smooth; set aside. Combine the panko, 1 tablespoon of the aquafaba, and 2 tablespoons of the olive oil in a separate bowl and set aside.

3. Make the meringue by adding the remaining 1/4 cup aquafaba and the cream of tartar to the bowl of a stand mixer. Using a whisk, vigorously whip the aquafaba for 10 seconds. Using the balloon whip attachment, whip the aquafaba on medium-low speed for 5 minutes. Increase the speed to medium-high and continue to whip until the meringue is climbing the side of the bowl and is forming stiff peaks (page 5), about 5 to 8 more minutes. Add the ketchup mixture, 1 tablespoon at a time, while the mixer is on medium-high.

4. Preheat the oven to 325°F. Add the chickpea mixture and the panko mixture to the whipped aquafaba and fold until well mixed. Set aside for 10 minutes to firm up. Divide the mixture into 2-tablespoon portions, then roll each portion firmly into a sphere. Place the meatballs on a baking sheet that has been coated with the remaining 1 1/2 tablespoons olive oil. Bake for 40 minutes, rotating the balls every 10 minutes; if simmering the meatballs in sauce for up to 5 minutes, bake for 50 minutes. These meatballs are best enjoyed freshly baked.

|||||||||||||||||||||||||||||||||||||||||||||||||||||||||||||||||||||||||||||||||||
Makes about 20 meatballs (4 to 6 servings)

NF, SF

SWEDISH MEATBALLS

|||||||||||||||||||||||||||||||||||||||||||||||||||||||||||||||||||||||||||||

These meatballs are denser than the Italian Meatballs, as Swedish meatballs are made using finely minced ingredients and no fillers, such as the breadcrumbs that keep the meatballs light and airy. Because the mixture is so dense, thanks to the legumes and mushrooms, the meringue provides a bit of much-needed lightness.

3 cups water
1 cup cooked chickpeas
1/3 cup green or brown lentils, picked over, rinsed, and drained
1 dried bay leaf
1 small onion, coarsely chopped
8 ounces button mushrooms, coarsely chopped
4 garlic cloves, coarsely chopped
2 tablespoons canola oil, other neutral oil, Butter (page 10), or store-bought nondairy butter
1 teaspoon sea salt
1/2 teaspoon ground allspice
1/4 teaspoon ground nutmeg
1/4 teaspoon ground black pepper
1 cup panko breadcrumbs
1/4 cup quick oats
1 tablespoon brown rice flour or unbleached all-purpose flour
1/4 cup aquafaba
1/8 teaspoon cream of tartar
Oil, for pan-frying
Swedish Meatball Gravy (recipe follows)
Lingonberry jam or whole cranberry sauce, for serving

1. Combine the water, chickpeas, lentils, and bay leaf in a medium saucepan over high heat. Bring to a boil, reduce to a simmer over medium heat, and cook until the lentils are tender, about 25 minutes. Remove and discard the bay leaf. Drain the chickpeas and lentils very well and set aside.

2. Add the onion, mushrooms, and garlic to a food processor. Pulse until finely chopped but not puréed. Heat the oil in a large skillet over medium-high heat. Add the onion mixture, salt, allspice, nutmeg, and black pepper, and cook until the onion mixture is golden brown and relatively dry.

3. Transfer the sautéed vegetables and drained chickpeas and lentils to the food processor. Add the panko, oats, and flour. Process until well combined and no whole lentils are visible. Taste and adjust the seasoning with salt and pepper.

4. Add the aquafaba and cream of tartar to the bowl of a stand mixer and use the balloon whip attachment or a whisk to whip the aquafaba for 20 seconds. Add the balloon whip to the machine and whip for 5 minutes on medium-low. Increase the speed to medium-high and whip until stiff peaks form (page 5), about 8 more minutes.

5. Preheat the oven to 350°F. Add the onion mixture to the whipped meringue and fold until no more whites are seen. Form the mixture into 1 1/2-tablespoon firm meatballs and set them on a baking sheet. Heat 1 tablespoon oil in the large skillet over medium heat and cook the meatballs until golden brown. Transfer the meatballs back to the baking sheet and bake them for 15 minutes. Remove them from the oven and set them aside to firm up for 5 to 10 minutes. Serve the meatballs with the gravy and the jam.

||||||||||||||||||||||||||||||||||||||||||||||||||||

Makes 20 meatballs (4 to 6 servings)

GFO, NF, SF

Gluten-Free Option: Use gluten-free breadcrumbs. To make the gravy, combine the milk, Worcestershire sauce, salt, pepper, and 3/4 cup of the broth in a medium saucepan and bring to a boil over medium heat. Omit the oil and flour. Combine the remaining 1/4 cup broth with 2 tablespoons cornstarch to form a slurry. Add the slurry and butter after the gravy has reduced a bit. Bring the gravy back to a simmer and cook gently just until thickened.

SWEDISH MEATBALL GRAVY
||||||||||||||||||||||||||||||||||||||||||||||||||||||||||||||||||||||

To make this gravy soy-free, use soy-free vegan butter, milk, and sour cream.

    3 tablespoons Butter (page 10) or store-bought nondairy butter
    3 tablespoons canola or other neutral oil
    1/3 cup unbleached all-purpose flour
    1 cup vegetable broth
    2 cups plain unsweetened nondairy milk
    2 tablespoons Worcestershire Sauce (page 23) or store-bought vegan Worcestershire sauce
    1/2 teaspoon sea salt
    Ground black pepper, to taste
    1/4 cup nondairy sour cream, optional

Heat the butter and oil in the large skillet. Add the flour and cook until it is golden brown, about 3 minutes, stirring constantly. Add the broth in a slow stream, while whisking the roux with a hand whisk. Add the milk slowly and whisk out any lumps. Add the Worcestershire sauce, salt, and black pepper and bring the gravy to a boil. Reduce the gravy to a simmer over medium heat and cook until the desired thickness is achieved, about 5 minutes. Whisk in the sour cream (if using).

MEATLOAF

Moist vegan meatloaf that stays together and is delicious is indeed possible. This recipe offers your choice of gravy or barbecue sauce for a topping. Using the food processor makes this loaf easier to put together. Make the meringue while the filling is cooking so it will be ready at the same time.

8 ounces cremini or button mushrooms
1 celery rib, cut into large chunks
1 medium carrot, cut into large chunks
1 medium onion, cut into large chunks
1 cup cooked chickpeas
4 garlic cloves, minced
4 tablespoons olive oil, divided
1 cup quick oats
1 teaspoon dried thyme
1 teaspoon dried sage
1 teaspoon sea salt
Ground black pepper, to taste
1 tablespoon nutritional yeast flakes

1 tablespoon Worcestershire Sauce
    (page 23) or store-bought vegan
    Worcestershire sauce
1 tablespoon reduced-sodium tamari
1 tablespoon Dijon mustard
2 tablespoons potato starch
1/4 cup aquafaba
1/4 teaspoon cream of tartar
Barbecue Sauce (recipe follows)
    (optional)
Meatloaf Gravy for serving, optional
    (recipe follows)

1. Preheat the oven to 350°F. Add the mushrooms, celery, carrot, onion, chickpeas, and garlic to a food processor. Pulse until everything is coarsely ground (this might need to be done in two batches). Heat 2 tablespoons of the olive oil in a large skillet over medium heat. Add the mushroom mixture, oats, thyme, sage, salt, black pepper, and nutritional yeast. Cook, stirring occasionally, until the mixture is golden brown and dry, about 10 to 12 minutes.

2. Deglaze the skillet with the Worcestershire sauce, tamari, and mustard. Cook until the liquid evaporates, about 2 minutes. Remove the skillet from the heat and add the potato starch. Mix well.

3. Add the aquafaba and cream of tartar to the bowl of a stand mixer. Using a whisk, vigorously whip the aquafaba for 10 seconds. Using the balloon whip attachment, whip the aquafaba on medium-low speed for 5 minutes. Increase the speed to medium-high and continue to whip for another 3 to 4 minutes, or until the meringue can hold firm peaks (page 5). Fold the meringue into the meatloaf mixture until no more foam is visible.

4. Add the remaining 2 tablespoons olive oil to a 9-inch loaf pan and rotate the pan to evenly coat it with the oil. Transfer the meatloaf mixture to the loaf pan, and press down gently. Bake for 70 minutes. If using barbecue sauce, brush the loaf with the sauce after it has baked for 50 minutes. Remove the meatloaf from the oven and allow it to cool for about 10 minutes to firm up. Slice and serve with Meatloaf Gravy, if using.

IIIIIIIIIIIIIIIIIIIIIIIIIIIII

Makes 4 servings

GF, NF, SFO

Soy-Free Option: Omit the tamari. Add 1 tablespoon coconut aminos and 1/8 teaspoon sea salt.

Barbecue Sauce: In a small bowl, combine 1/4 cup ketchup, 1 tablespoon apple cider vinegar, 1 teaspoon packed Light Brown Sugar (page 23) or store-bought brown sugar, 1/4 teaspoon garlic powder, and a pinch salt.

Meatloaf Gravy: Make the Swedish Meatball Gravy (page 61), but reduce the butter and oil to 1 1/2 table-spoons each. Reduce the flour to 3 tablespoons and add 1/2 teaspoon dried parsley. Reduce the amount of milk to 1/2 cup, the Worcestershire sauce to 1 tablespoon, and season with salt and pepper to taste. Keep the same amount of broth. Omit the sour cream.

HOT CROSS BUNS

These are the sweet, spiced buns traditionally served at the end of Lent. The buns are laced with dried fruit and decorated with a cross of glaze. Historically, these buns had been unlawful to sell on any but religious days, but now they are available year-round. Some recipes include eggs, others don't, but the aquafaba in these make for a light, fluffy bun. See Proofing dough (page 166).

Dough
1 cup warm nondairy milk (not hotter than 110°F)
2 1/4 teaspoons dry active yeast
1/4 cup aquafaba
1/4 cup canola or other neutral oil
1/4 cup granulated organic sugar
1 teaspoon pure vanilla extract
2 teaspoons psyllium husk powder
1 teaspoon sea salt
1/2 teaspoon ground cinnamon
1/4 teaspoon ground cardamom

1/4 teaspoon ground nutmeg
3 3/4 cups unbleached all-purpose flour
1/2 cup dried raisins, currants, cherries, or cranberries

Aquafaba Wash
1/4 cup aquafaba
1/2 teaspoon arrowroot or cornstarch

Lemon Glaze
2/3 cup confectioners' sugar, sifted
2 1/2 to 2 3/4 teaspoons fresh lemon juice

1. **Dough:** Combine the milk and yeast in the bowl of a stand mixer or a large bowl. Set aside for 5 minutes to proof. Combine the aquafaba, oil, sugar, vanilla, psyllium husk powder, salt, cinnamon, cardamom, and nutmeg in a small bowl or measuring cup. Set aside to thicken for 4 minutes. Add this to the milk mixture. Add the flour and raisins and knead on low speed (or with a wooden spoon) until incorporated. Increase the speed to medium and knead for 5 minutes. The dough should be soft and tacky.

2. Transfer the dough to an oiled bowl, cover the bowl, and let the dough rise in a warm place until doubled, about 2 hours. Gently deflate the dough and divide it into 12 equal portions. Roll each portion into a ball and place it on an oiled baking sheet (or silicone mat–lined baking sheet). Cover the buns and let them rise until doubled, about 30 to 45 minutes. Preheat the oven to 375°F.

3. **Aquafaba Wash:** Combine the aquafaba and arrowroot or cornstarch in a small saucepan. Cook over medium heat just until thickened. Remove and set aside to cool a bit.

4. Brush the buns with the aquafaba wash and bake them until they are golden brown and sound hollow when thumped on the bottom, about 20 minutes.

5. **Lemon Glaze:** Combine the confectioners' sugar and lemon juice in a small bowl; reserve 1/4 teaspoon of juice to make sure the glaze isn't too watery. Add the extra juice if needed. Mix well using a whisk and decorate the buns as desired, traditionally by using the glaze to draw a cross through the center of each bun.

Makes 12 buns

NF, SF

GLUTEN-FREE ARTISAN BREAD

It is important to measure gluten-free flour appropriately. Mix the container of flour with a whisk or butter knife and, using a spoon, scoop the flour into the measuring cup until it is overfilled. Using the back of the butter knife, scrape away any excess flour back into the container. This gluten-free bread uses no xanthan gum.

　　1/2 cup warm aquafaba (not hotter than 110°F)
　　3 teaspoons dry active yeast
　　2 teaspoons granulated organic sugar
　　2 tablespoons olive oil
　　1 teaspoon psyllium husk powder
　　1 1/4 cups white rice flour
　　1 cup tapioca starch
　　1/2 cup sweet sorghum flour
　　1/4 cup chickpea flour
　　1 teaspoon sea salt
　　1 cup water, warmed to room temperature

1. Combine the aquafaba, yeast, and sugar in a small bowl. Set the mixture aside for 5 minutes to proof. Combine the olive oil and psyllium husk powder in a small container and mix well. Set aside.

2. Sift together the rice flour, tapioca starch, sorghum flour, chickpea flour, and salt into a medium bowl. Add the bloomed yeast mixture, the oil mixture, and the water. Mix well to combine using a whisk. The mixture will seem very thin for bread dough, but it will thicken up considerably as it proofs. Cover the bowl containing the dough with a plate or another bowl and set aside for 2 hours to grow the yeast.

3. Preheat the oven to 400°F with a pan of hot water on the bottom rack of the oven. Prepare a baking sheet with parchment paper or a silicone mat. Transfer the thickened dough to the baking sheet and shape it into the desired form using wet hands; the dough will still be very loose and sticky, but do not add more flour. Shape the dough long, tall, and thin for a bâtarde-style loaf, wide and short for an Italian-style loaf, or round and tall for a boule-style loaf. Brush with aquafaba wash (page 64) or sprinkle with rice flour. Make two or three 1-inch deep slashes in the bread to allow air to escape.

4. Bake the bread for about 25 to 35 minutes, or until rich golden brown and the inside temperature is at least 205°F. Allow the bread to thoroughly cool before cutting into it, as gluten-free bread needs time to firm up.

Makes 1 loaf

GF, NF, SF

CHALLAH

This lightly sweet, rich bread is traditionally made with egg yolks and features a beautiful braid and a golden egg-wash crust. This vegan version is made using aquafaba in the loaf and an aquafaba wash to finish it off. The more braids you have in the bread, the longer it will take to bake (up to four more minutes). See Proofing dough (page 166).

Dough
3/4 cup warm water (not hotter than 110°F)
6 tablespoons maple syrup, divided
1 tablespoon dry active yeast
6 tablespoons canola or other neutral oil
5 3/4 cups unbleached all-purpose flour
2 teaspoons sea salt
2 pinches turmeric
1/2 cup aquafaba

Aquafaba Wash
1/4 cup aquafaba
1/2 teaspoon arrowroot or cornstarch

1. **Dough:** Combine the water, 1 tablespoon of the maple syrup, and yeast in a medium bowl. Set aside for 5 minutes to proof. Add the remaining 5 tablespoons of the maple syrup and oil.

2. Combine the flour, salt, and turmeric in a separate medium bowl and set aside.

3. Add the aquafaba to a large bowl or the bowl of a stand mixer and, using a whisk, beat the aquafaba until it is light and frothy, about 1 minute. Add the yeast mixture and about 4 cups of the flour mixture. Knead the dough in the stand mixer or using a large wooden spoon. Mix well and add the rest of the flour mixture as needed to create a firm dough; try adding most, if not all, of the flour mixture. Knead the dough for 10 minutes to develop the gluten. The dough should be smooth and push back when poked.

4. Transfer the dough to a lightly oiled bowl, cover the bowl, and let the dough rise in a warm place until doubled, about 1 hour. Deflate the dough and let it rise again until doubled, about another hour. Divide the dough in two and divide each half into three, four, or six pieces, depending on how you would like to braid the dough. Keep the pieces covered until ready to use.

5. Roll each portion of dough into a 12-inch long, tapered rope. Braid half the ropes into a challah loaf. Set the braided dough on a baking sheet, repeat the process with the other half of the ropes, and cover each loaf with a towel. Let the dough rise in a warm place for 40 minutes.

6. **Aquafaba Wash:** Combine the aquafaba and arrowroot or cornstarch in small saucepan. Cook over medium heat just until thickened. Cool slightly before use. (For a sweeter, slightly sticky wash, combine 3 tablespoons aquafaba with 1 tablespoon maple syrup; no need to heat the maple syrup mixture before use.)

7. Preheat the oven to 350°F. Brush the aquafaba wash all over the bread and bake for 10 minutes. Brush

the bread with the wash again, continue to bake for about 20 to 25 more minutes, and check the bread for doneness. If the bread is browning too quickly, tent it with foil or continue to bake it upside down. Tap on the bottom of the bread; if it sounds hollow, it is probably ready. Let the challah cool before serving.

‖‖‖‖‖‖‖‖‖‖‖‖‖‖‖‖‖‖‖‖
Makes 2 loaves

NF, SF

BRIOCHE

Brioche isn't an everyday bread, but it certainly is a magnificent once-in-a-while bread. Don't be surprised, though, if you are asked to make it often. The bread is flaky, buttery, and rich. It tastes great toasted or used to make cinnamon rolls. It might sound like an intimidating bread to make, but the machine does most of the work for you. See Proofing dough on page 166 for some helpful tips. For a soy-free version, choose a soy-free nondairy butter.

Sponge
8 tablespoons warm aquafaba (not hotter than 110°F)
1 cup warm plain unsweetened nondairy milk (not hotter than 110°F)
1 tablespoon dry active yeast
1 cup unbleached all-purpose flour
2 teaspoons psyllium husk powder

Dough
1/3 cup granulated organic sugar
3 cups unbleached all-purpose flour
1 teaspoon sea salt
3/4 cup (1 1/2 sticks) cold nondairy butter

Aquafaba Wash
1/4 cup aquafaba
1/2 teaspoon arrowroot or cornstarch

1. **Sponge:** Combine the aquafaba, milk, yeast, flour, and psyllium husk powder in the bowl of a stand mixer. Mix well using the balloon whip attachment. Cover the bowl and set aside to proof for 30 minutes.

2. **Dough:** Add the sugar to the aquafaba mixture and mix. Combine the flour and salt in a medium bowl, mixing well. Remove the whip attachment and add the dough hook attachment. With the mixer running, add the flour mixture slowly, about 2 tablespoons at a time. With the mixer on low, knead the dough for 15 minutes. Do not skip this step; it is what gives the bread its characteristic texture.

3. After 15 minutes, add the cold butter about 2 tablespoons at a time. Your dough will break, but it will recombine with more kneading. After all the butter has been added, continue to knead for another 5 to 10 minutes. If, after 5 minutes, the dough seems to not want to recombine, add up to 2 tablespoons of flour. The dough will be very sticky and loose.

4. Transfer the dough to a well-oiled medium bowl, cover the bowl, and set it in a warm place to rise for 2 hours. Deflate the dough by pinching it in a half dozen places. Fold the dough over itself a few times, cover well, and let it rise in the refrigerator for 12 to 16 hours.

5. Prepare 2 (9-inch) loaf pans by spraying them well with oil or rubbing them with butter. Remove the dough from the refrigerator and cut the dough in half. If you are baking the bread one loaf at a time, store the other half of the dough in the refrigerator. Transfer the half-portion of the dough to a lightly floured work surface and form it into a rectangle. Fold it into thirds one way and then into thirds the other way.

Flatten the dough again and fold it into thirds about the size of your loaf pan. Add the loaf to the prepared pan (seam-side down), spray it with oil, cover it with wax paper and a kitchen towel, and set it aside in a warm place to double in size, about 2 hours. Preheat the oven to 375°F.

6. **Aquafaba Wash:** Combine the aquafaba and arrowroot or cornstarch in small saucepan. Cook the mixture over medium heat just until thickened. Cool slightly before use. Brush the loaf with the aquafaba wash. Bake the bread for 30 to 35 minutes, or until golden brown and the internal temperature is 205°F. Tent the loaf with foil if it is browning too fast.

7. Once the loaf is baked, remove it from the pan immediately and cool it on a rack until it is warm. Brioche is best fresh and slightly warm but will keep for a few days if stored well covered in an airtight container.

||||||||||||||||||||||||||||||
Makes 2 loaves

NF, SFO

SWEETS FROM THE PANTRY

This chapter contains sweet recipes that use ingredients from your pantry and are not baked, except for a supplemental recipe, such as pie crust. You will find candies, such as Nougat and Fantasy Fudge; pies, such as Lemon Meringue and Mississippi Mud; and a rich chocolate mousse, as well as rich, creamy ice creams.

Fried Doughnuts 72

Featherlight Chocolate Mousse 73

Nougat 76

Marshmallow Crème 78

Puffed Rice Treat Bars 79

Marshmallows 82

Fantasy Fudge 84

Mississippi Mud Pie 87

Sweet Whipped Topping 88

Lemon Meringue Pie 90

Coconut-Key Lime Cream Pie 95

Chocolate Ice Cream 96

Berry Swirl-Coconut Ice Cream 98

Caramel-Praline Cashew Ice Cream 100

FRIED DOUGHNUTS

|||||||||||||||||||||||||||||||||||||||||||||||||||||||||||||||||||||||||||||||||||||||

Doughnuts that are light, fluffy, and airy are only found in shops, not in home kitchens. Until now. While there are a few baked doughnuts in the breakfast chapter, I couldn't resist offering you a decadent dessert doughnut. Of course, who am I to judge when you enjoy it? These doughnuts can be rolled in sugar, doused with ganache (page 116), or sprinkled with cinnamon. See Proofing dough (page 166).

- **1/2 cup nondairy milk**
- **1/4 cup granulated organic sugar**
- **1/4 cup aquafaba**
- **3 tablespoons nondairy butter**
- **2 1/4 teaspoons dry active yeast**
- **2 1/2 cups unbleached all-purpose flour, divided**
- **High-heat oil, for frying**

1. Combine the milk, sugar, aquafaba, and butter in a medium saucepan over medium heat. Stir and cook just until the sugar and butter dissolve. Transfer the milk mixture to a large bowl and cool to between 100°F and 110°F. Add the yeast and proof for 5 minutes. Add 2 1/4 cups of the flour and gently knead to combine. Transfer the dough to a lightly floured work surface and gently knead into a smooth, tacky dough. Add more flour if the dough is too sticky, but try not to add too much more or knead with a heavy hand to avoid making the dough tough. Oil the bowl and add the dough. Turn to coat the dough with oil and cover. Set aside to double in size, about 2 hours.

2. Gently deflate the dough and transfer it to a lightly floured work surface. Roll the dough out to a 1/2-inch thickness. Using a doughnut cutter (or two biscuit cutters, one smaller than the other), cut the dough into round doughnuts. Alternatively, cut the doughnuts into squares. Transfer the doughnuts to a lightly floured baking sheet. Cover the doughnuts and let them rise until doubled in size, about 30 minutes to 1 hour.

3. Heat 2 inches of oil in a large saucepan over medium to medium-high heat. Heat the oil to 375°F. When the oil is hot enough, carefully add a few doughnuts. Cook each side of the doughnuts until golden brown, 30 to 40 seconds per side. Remove the doughnuts from the oil and transfer them to a baking sheet lined with paper towels to drain. Use a pastry bag and 1/4-inch tip to fill the doughnuts with chocolate ganache (page 116), roll them in confectioners' sugar, or roll them in granulated sugar or dip them in the chocolate glaze used in the Baked Chocolate Doughnuts (page 27) or the sugar glaze in the Baked Apple Cider Doughnut recipe (page 28), using milk instead of apple cider to make the glaze. Enjoy soon after frying.

|||||||||||||||||||||||||||||||||

Makes 8 doughnuts

NF, SFO

Soy-Free Option: Use soy-free vegan butter.

FEATHERLIGHT CHOCOLATE MOUSSE

This is one of the first recipes that you should make when you first start working with aquafaba because it is relatively easy and quick and there is a high reward. Naturally, it will be one you will make over and over again, but as a beginner, this is definitely a standout. Check out Whipping Aquafaba (page 5) for instructions regarding peaks of a meringue.

1/2 cup aquafaba
1/8 teaspoon cream of tartar
2 tablespoons granulated organic sugar
1/2 cup nondairy semisweet chocolate chips
1 tablespoon plain unsweetened nondairy milk
2 teaspoons cherry extract or 1 teaspoon pure vanilla extract
2 pinches sea salt

1. Add the aquafaba and cream of tartar to the bowl of a stand mixer. Using a whisk, whip the aquafaba for 10 seconds. Using a balloon whip attachment, whip the aquafaba on medium speed for 5 minutes. Increase the speed to medium-high and continue to whip for another 5 to 8 minutes, or until the aquafaba can hold stiff peaks (page 5) and is climbing the side of the bowl. Add the sugar, 1 tablespoon at a time, over the course of 1 minute and continue to whip for an additional 4 to 5 minutes, or until the sugar has dissolved.

2. Combine the chocolate chips, milk, extract, and salt in a glass or metal bowl that will fit over a medium saucepan of water. Heat the water over medium heat and cook until the chocolate in the bowl melts, about 6 minutes. Remove the bowl from the saucepan and allow the chocolate to cool to room temperature, about 10 minutes.

3. Transfer a large scoop of the meringue to the cooled chocolate and mix well. Transfer all of this tempered chocolate to the mixer bowl and gently fold to combine. Scoop the mousse into glasses and chill in the refrigerator until firm, about 8 hours.

Makes 3 1/2 cups

GF, NF, SF

Candy Making: Tips, Tricks, and Techniques

Candy making is a bit of an art and a whole lot of science.

The object of cooking sugar and water together is to add as much sugar into the solution of simple syrup as is desired by a specific recipe. When sugar is dissolved into water, a solution is created. However, you can only add just so much sugar to a specific amount of water. Raising the temperature of the solution will allow more sugar to dissolve in a certain amount of water because there is less water in the solution as the water evaporates, creating a supersaturated solution. The temperature of the syrup will determine how saturated your solution will be. This is why an accurate candy thermometer is essential.

Sugar will cool to different concentrations as it reaches different temperatures. For instance, cooking simple syrup to 235°F will create a candy that cools to the texture of soft balls, meaning that when a drop of hot syrup is placed in cold water it can be rolled into a ball and the ball will feel soft. Cooking that same syrup to 270°F instead will create a candy that cools to the texture of hard but pliable candy. This is soft crack, meaning that when a drop of hot syrup is placed in cold water it will form threads that are pliable but not brittle.

However, supersaturated solutions are very unstable and a single incident (such as a stray sugar crystal or movement of the pan) can send the whole pot of supersaturated solution into a tailspin of crystallization; before you know it, that batch of smooth candy has reverted to solid crystals. While that is a desired effect for some candy (such as fudge), for other candies (such as caramel) it is not. How you cook your syrup and how you treat it will determine the texture of your final, cooled candy.

Adding another type of sugar to the pot of cooking syrup can interfere with the crystallization and help keep your syrup a supersaturated solution. This is why many recipes call for invert syrups such as corn syrup or glucose syrup to be added. Corn syrup and glucose syrup are different kinds of sugar and get in between the sucrose molecules, which can, if they collide, cause the domino effect of crystallization. With the help of an invert syrup and a few tips in mind, you can keep your syrup clear and smooth.

Things to Keep in Mind When Making Candy

- **Be aware of humidity.** The additional water in the air can interfere with candy making. My rule of thumb is that I don't attempt candy making on humid or overcast days. An old tale it is, but I've ruined more than a few batches of fudge on rainy days—so I give some credence to the lore.

- **Use a clean saucepan.** A stray dust particle can set the process of crystallization in motion. Rinse your saucepan and lid before adding the water and sugar.

- **Use light-colored organic sugar.** The darker your sugar, the easier it will burn.

- **Use the correct heating element.** Your burner should fit the size of the pot you are cooking your syrup in. If your burner is smaller than your pot, the syrup will have hot and cold spots. These hot and cold spots can also happen when additional ingredients, such as agar, are cooked with the water and sugar.

- **Keep your thermometer clean and warm.** Your thermometer and the attachment that fits on the saucepan should be clean and warm. A cold thermometer can start crystallization because it sends a shock of cold through the syrup.

- **Stir until all the sugar melts.** Make sure all the sugar is melted before the syrup comes to a boil. If there are stray sugar crystals that haven't melted, they can be the trigger for crystallization.

- **Do not stir the syrup once it's boiling.** Once your syrup is at a boil, add a lid and cook the syrup for three minutes. This will cause steam to turn back to water and drip onto the sides of the saucepan, washing down any stray sugar crystals. After your syrup is at a boil, do not stir it again, unless specified in a recipe (such as fudge).

- **Wash the sides of your pan.** Using hot water and a silicone or natural brush, wash down the sides of the pan as the syrup cooks to remove any sugar that may still be hanging around. Dip the brush often in clean water to remove sugar sticking to the brush itself. Because the syrup has been cooked with a lid trapping the evaporating liquid, most of the sugar will have been washed away already, but you can take this extra precaution if you find it necessary because your candy has crystallized in the past.

- **Do not jostle or move the pan until the sugar is ready.** Do not move your pan or jostle it while it is cooking, except to gently add the thermometer. Once the syrup has reached temperature (usually you can remove it from the heat a degree before it does, as the carry-over heat will raise the temperature further), gently move the pan from the heat and allow it to cool for at least fifteen minutes before removing the thermometer or moving the candy, unless otherwise specified in a recipe.

- **Do not scrape syrup or candy from the pan.** When you are pouring your syrup or candy into another container or vessel, resist the urge to scrape the pan clean. Scraping any syrup from the pan can bring stray solidified sugar with it and cause crystallization. Pour as much out as you can, but do not scrape the rest.

Be careful when adding hot syrup to meringue. In the recipes, I instruct you to carefully add the hot syrup to the meringue while the machine is whipping. It is important to aim for the space between the bowl and the whisk, but that isn't always possible. It is better to aim for the bowl than the whisk, because the whisk will pull the syrup into threads. If you can, aim for the side of the bowl with some meringue on it and slowly pour the syrup in a very thin stream. Try to pour in the same spot so that even if some of the syrup hardens onto the side of the bowl, only a small amount will harden and only in that one spot. It goes without saying to handle the hot syrup very carefully. Slow the machine down when you start to add the syrup, and then increase the speed as more syrup is added.

It is very important to note that you should only add hot syrup to bowls that are heat-proof, preferably a stainless steel bowl, especially when whipping hot syrup into meringue. When making recipes with hot syrup and meringue, prepare the meringue first and then the syrup. The meringue can continue to be whipped for up to 20 minutes or longer to keep the peaks stiff, especially if it has no agar in it (see page 166). The hot syrup cannot be set aside to wait for the meringue to be whipped.

NOUGAT

This is a softer nougat that stretches when bitten into. As with all candy, do not make this on humid or rainy days, since sugar is hydroscopic and will absorb any water in the air. If you'd like a harder nougat, reduce the amount of Reduced Aquafaba to 2 tablespoons and use a hand mixer to whip it instead of a stand mixer; it will take longer to achieve the proper peaks using a hand mixer.

Meringue
1/4 cup cold Reduced Aquafaba (page 3)
2 tablespoons granulated organic sugar
1/4 teaspoon cream of tartar

Sugar Syrup
1 1/2 cups granulated organic sugar
3/4 cup Honey Substitute (page 80)
2 tablespoons water

Add-Ins
1 1/2 cups toasted nuts (almonds, pistachios, pepitas, or pecans) and/or dried fruit (cherries, chopped apricots, or cranberries), warm
1 teaspoon lemon zest
1 teaspoon pure vanilla extract

1. Before preparing the recipe, please read the Candy Making section (page 74). Prepare a 9- x 5-inch baking sheet with a 15- x 20-inch piece of parchment paper. Spray the parchment paper well with oil and set aside. Prepare the add-ins and place them next to the meringue.

2. Meringue: In the bowl of a stand mixer, add the reduced aquafaba, sugar, and cream of tartar. Use a whisk or the balloon whip attachment to hand-whip the aquafaba for 10 seconds. Add the balloon whip to the machine or use a hand mixer to whip the aquafaba for 5 minutes at medium-low speed. Increase the speed to medium-high and continue to whip until stiff peaks (page 5) form, about 10 to 12 minutes.

3. Sugar syrup: In a medium heavy-bottomed saucepan combine the sugar, honey substitute, and water. Bring the sugar syrup to a boil over medium-high heat (this will take a few minutes), stirring to melt the sugar. Once the sugar is melted, reduce the heat to medium, and cover the saucepan with a tight-fitting lid. Cook for 3 minutes. Remove the lid, wash the sides of the pan with water, and attach a candy thermometer; do not stir again. Cook the syrup until it reaches 290°F (high soft-crack stage). Turn off the heat and allow the sugar syrup to cool a few degrees; do not move or jiggle the pan until then.

4. Once the meringue is ready, slow the machine and add the sugar syrup slowly in a steady stream, trying not to touch the whisk. Once all the syrup has been added, increase the speed to medium-high and whip for 4 minutes; the sides of the bowl should be warm to the touch.

5. Remove the bowl from the machine and stir in the warm nuts, fruit, zest, and vanilla. Quickly add the Nougat to the oiled parchment and, using the paper, form it into a rectangle. Encase the nougat completely in the parchment. Use a flat-bottomed pan to flatten it to a 1/2-inch thickness. Set the nougat in the refrigerator to harden for 4 to 6 hours.

6. Remove the parchment and cut the Nougat into 1/2-inch cubes. Wrap each piece of candy in wax paper and store them in an airtight container in the refrigerator for up to 4 weeks.

|||||||||||||||||||||||||||||||||||||||||||||||||||||||||||||

Makes 30 (1/2-inch) candy pieces

GF, NFO, SF

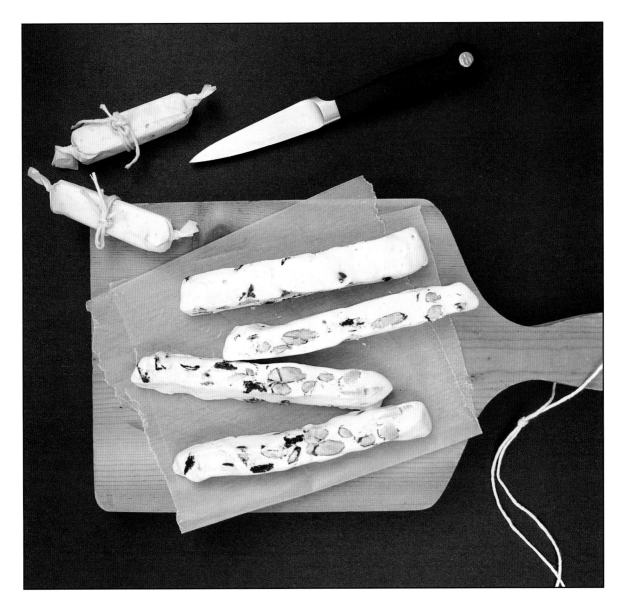

MARSHMALLOW CRÈME

||||||||||||||||||||||||||||||||||||||||||||||||||||||||||||||||||||||||||||||||||||||||||||||||

It is eerie how much this tastes and feels like nonvegan marshmallow crème. Constanze Reichardt of SeitanIsMyMotor.com, a fabulous baker in her own right, was one of the first to start experimenting with aquafaba, and she made marshmallow crème that looked like the real thing. My version is not the same as the popular vegan marshmallow crème but is more like the nonvegan version in a jar. You can enjoy this on toast with peanut butter, in hot chocolate, or use it to make fudge. In fact, if it crystallizes, it still makes great fudge.

Meringue
1/2 cup aquafaba
1/2 teaspoon xanthan gum
1/4 teaspoon cream of tartar

Syrup
1/2 cup water
1/2 cup Glucose Syrup (page 80) or light corn syrup
1 1/2 cups granulated organic sugar
1 teaspoon pure vanilla extract

1. See the Candy Making section (page 74) before preparing the recipe.

2. Meringue: Add the aquafaba, xanthan gum, and cream of tartar to the bowl of a stand mixer. Using a whisk, whip the aquafaba for 10 seconds. Using a balloon whip attachment, whip the aquafaba on medium speed for 5 minutes. Increase the speed to medium-high and continue to whip for another 7 minutes, or until the aquafaba can hold stiff peaks (page 5).

3. Syrup: Combine the water, glucose syrup, and sugar in a heavy-bottomed medium saucepan, Bring the syrup to a boil over medium-high heat (this will take a few minutes), stirring to melt the sugar, reduce the heat to medium, and cover with a tight-fitting lid. Cook for 3 minutes. Remove the lid, wash the sides of the pan with water, and attach a candy thermometer; do not stir again. Cook the syrup until it reaches 260°F (soft-crack stage). Turn off the heat and allow the sugar syrup to cool a few degrees; do not move or jiggle the pan until then.

4. Once the meringue is ready, slow the machine and add the sugar syrup slowly in a steady stream, trying not to touch the sides of the bowl or the whisk. Once all the syrup has been added, increase the speed to medium-high and whip for 10 minutes; the sides of the bowl should become lukewarm by the time the mixture is done whipping. Add the vanilla during the last 30 seconds of whipping. Allow the marshmallow crème to cool completely and transfer it to an airtight container stored in the pantry for up to 2 weeks.

||||||||||||||||||||||||||||||||||||||||

Makes about 3 cups

GF, NF, SF

PUFFED RICE TREAT BARS

After you make the marshmallow recipe on page 82, you might want to use some of them to make these fun retro snack bars.

1 tablespoon Butter (page 10) or store-bought nondairy butter
10 ounces Marshmallows (page 82), chopped (about 2 cups)
3 cups crispy puffed rice cereal

Melt the butter in a medium saucepan over medium heat. Add the marshmallows and cook, stirring constantly until completely melted. Remove the marshmallow mixture from the heat and stir in the cereal. Transfer the mixture to an oiled 9-inch loaf pan and, using a piece of parchment paper, push down firmly and smooth out the cereal. Cool until firm. Cut the firm rice cereal into about 3 1/2- x 1-inch bars. These are best enjoyed the same day they're made, but they will keep stored in an airtight container for a few days.

Makes about 9 bars

GF, NF, SFO

Soy-Free Option: Use soy-free butter to make this soy-free.

How to Calibrate Your Thermometer

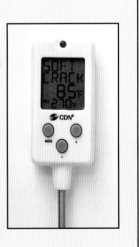

If you suspect that your thermometer is not accurate, bring a saucepan of water to a boil. Keep the water at a rolling boil, with bubbles that are constant. Add a thermometer and test the temperature after five minutes, making sure that the probe is not touching the bottom or sides of the pot. If your thermometer reads 212°F, your thermometer is accurate. If the temperature is off, adjust the reading by adding or subtracting the amount needed when you use it during candy making. Write down the discrepancy and keep the note with the thermometer.

If your sugar burns or your syrup sticks in the pan, don't worry—your pan is not lost. Normal cooked syrup will come off with just a soak of hot water, but even if your sugar burns, simply add water to cover the burned sugar and boil it until the sugar dissolves.

GLUCOSE SYRUP TWO WAYS

Honey Substitute

Reducing white grape juice or apple juice with sugar and cream of tartar makes quite a remarkable version of honey. Upon making it again (and no doubt you will), you can even reduce it to make it thicker or thinner, according to your taste.

> **2 cups filtered white grape juice or apple juice**
> **1 3/4 cups granulated organic sugar**
> **1/2 teaspoon cream of tartar**

1. See the Candy Making section (page 74) before preparing the recipe. Combine the juice, sugar, and cream of tartar in a heavy-bottomed medium saucepan; stir well. Bring the mixture to a boil over medium heat, stirring to melt the sugar. Cover the saucepan with a tight-fitting lid and cook for 3 minutes to wash the sides of any stray sugar crystals. Remove the lid and attach a candy thermometer; do not stir again. Reduce the heat to medium-low and cook the syrup until it reaches 240°F.

2. Gently remove the saucepan from the heat and let the syrup cool completely before transferring it to clean, clear 1/2-pint mason jars. Store the jars in a cool, dry place where they will be moved very little, as any movement can set off crystallization. To use, heat the jar in a pan of hot water or in the microwave to soften enough to use. Make sure the syrup has not begun crystallization before using it in a candy recipe by examining the jar for signs of crystallized sugar.

Makes about 1 3/4 cups

GF, NF, SF

Glucose Syrup (Corn Syrup Substitute)

Whether known as glucose syrup or corn syrup, there are times when you need it in a recipe and either can't find it or would rather not use it. Since using glucose syrup can be a necessity, based on the recipe, it is important to note that this syrup will satisfy those requirements. In the presence of acid, sugar will break apart into its two different molecules—fructose and glucose—hence making it possible to add a completely different sugar molecule to sugar syrup. The advantage there is that in the presence of an alien sugar molecule, regular sugar will find it more difficult to crystallize.

> **2 cups granulated organic sugar**
> **3/4 cup water**
> **1 teaspoon cream of tartar**
> **Pinch salt**

1. See the Candy Making section (page 74) before preparing the recipe. Combine the sugar, water, cream of tartar, and salt in a heavy-bottomed medium saucepan; stir well. Bring the mixture to a boil over medium heat, stirring to melt the sugar. Cover the saucepan with a tight-fitting lid and cook for 3 minutes to wash the sides of any stray sugar crystals.

2. Remove the lid and attach a candy thermometer; do not stir again. Reduce the heat to medium-low and cook the syrup until it reaches 240°F.

3. Gently remove the saucepan from the heat and let the syrup cool completely before transferring it to clean, clear 1/2-pint mason jars. Store the jars in a cool, dry place where they will be moved very little, as any movement can set off crystallization. To use, heat the jar in a pan of hot water or in the microwave to soften enough to use. Make sure the syrup has not begun crystallization before using it in a candy recipe by examining the jar for signs of crystallized sugar.

||||||||||||||||||||||||||||||||||||||||||||||||

Makes about 1 3/4 cups

GF, NF, SF

MARSHMALLOWS

|||||||||||||||||||||||||||||||||||||||||||||||||||||||||||||||||||||||||||||||

Light, fluffy, spongy, and airy. All the texture of a marshmallow is here. Use them in s'mores, chop them small for hot chocolate, or make crispy rice treats (page 79). As with all homemade marshmallows, this is softer than commercial brands, but definitely tastier. Kelly Peloza, author of *The Vegan Cookie Connoisseur* and blogger at SeitanBeatsYourMeat.com, inspired me to make marshmallows when she posted her creation of dried vegan mini marshmallows that are the perfect addition to cold cereal. I instantly knew it was, indeed, possible to make homemade vegan marshmallows.

> 1/4 cup arrowroot or cornstarch
> 1/2 cup confectioners' sugar
>
> **Meringue**
> 1/2 cup aquafaba
> 1/2 teaspoon xanthan gum
> 1/4 teaspoon cream of tartar
>
> **Syrup**
> 1/4 cup water
> 2 teaspoons agar powder
> 1/2 cup Glucose Syrup (page 80) or light corn syrup
> 1 1/2 cups granulated organic sugar
> 2 tablespoons tapioca starch
> 2 teaspoons pure vanilla extract

1. See the Candy Making section (page 74) before preparing the recipe.

2. Sift together the arrowroot or cornstarch and confectioners' sugar. Prepare an 8- x 8-inch baking pan by sifting 1/4 cup of the confectioners' sugar mixture all over the bottom of the pan. Set aside.

3. **Meringue:** Add the aquafaba, xanthan gum, and cream of tartar to the bowl of a stand mixer. Using a whisk, whip the aquafaba for 10 seconds. Using a balloon whip attachment, whip the aquafaba on medium speed for 5 minutes. Increase the speed to medium-high and continue to whip for another 7 minutes, or until the aquafaba can hold stiff peaks (page 5).

4. **Syrup:** Combine the water and agar in a heavy-bottomed medium saucepan and set the mixture aside to soften for 3 minutes. Add the glucose syrup carefully to the middle of the pan. Add the sugar to the middle of the liquid, avoiding the sides of the pan. Stir until all the sugar dissolves over medium-high heat and bring the mixture to a boil (this will take a few minutes). Reduce the heat to medium and cover the saucepan with a tight-fitting lid. Cook for 3 minutes. Remove the lid, wash the sides of the pan with water, and attach a candy thermometer; do not stir again. Cook the syrup until it reaches 252°F to 254°F (hard-ball stage). Without jiggling the saucepan, carefully move it off the heat and allow the sugar syrup to cool a few degrees or until it is no longer bubbling.

5. Once the meringue is ready, slow the machine and add the sugar syrup slowly in a steady stream, trying not to touch the sides of the bowl or the whisk. Once all the syrup has been added, sift in the tapioca starch

using a small strainer. Increase the speed to medium-high and whip for 10 minutes; the sides of the bowl should become lukewarm by the time the mixture is done whipping. Add the vanilla during the last minute of whipping.

6. Transfer the marshmallow mixture to the prepared baking pan and smooth it out as much as possible. Sift on 2 tablespoons of the confectioners' sugar mixture. Set the marshmallow mixture aside in the refrigerator to firm up overnight. Cut the firm mixture into 1- x 1-inch squares and roll them in the confectioners' sugar mixture. Store the marshmallows in an airtight container in layers separated with wax paper in the refrigerator for up to 2 weeks.

||||||||||||||||||||||||||||||||||||||||||||||||||||||||||||||||||
Makes 64 (1- x 1-inch) marshmallows

GF, SF, NF

FANTASY FUDGE

||||||||||||||||||||||||||||||||||||||||||||||||||||||||||||||||

This is the kind of fudge that you have to stir constantly to achieve the perfect texture. Because of the addition of vegan milk and vegan butter, the fudge would burn if prepared the traditional way of reducing the temperature to 110°F before stirring. The Marshmallow Crème gives this a milk chocolate taste and feel.

> 1 1/2 cups nondairy milk
> 1 1/4 cups granulated organic sugar
> 1/4 cup nondairy butter
> 1 cup bittersweet chocolate chips
> 3/4 cup Marshmallow Crème (page 78)

1. Prepare a 9-inch loaf pan with parchment paper. Set aside. Combine the milk, sugar, and butter in a tall, heavy-bottomed medium saucepan; the saucepan should be large enough to hold two to three times the contents of the ingredients. Stir the milk mixture well and bring it to a boil over medium heat. Attach a candy thermometer and stir continuously until the syrup reaches 236°F, about 30 minutes. The syrup will become very thick. It is important to stir constantly or the mixture will boil over or burn. (You may use a large saucepan to ensure that it doesn't boil over, but thermometers have a difficult time reading small amounts of liquid; the liquid will boil down considerably.)

2. Once the mixture is at temperature, add the chocolate chips but do not stir. Carefully transfer the syrup with the chocolate chips to the bowl of a stand mixer fitted with a paddle attachment. Mix on medium speed until the chocolate melts and the mixture is smooth, about 30 seconds. Add the marshmallow crème by the heaping tablespoonful as the fudge is mixing. Continue to mix the fudge until it is smooth and no longer shiny, about 4 minutes.

3. Transfer the fudge to the prepared pan and smooth the top. Set aside to firm up at least overnight. If the fudge is too soft for you, leave it at room temperature until it dries out more. When the fudge is at your ideal texture, cut it and store it in an airtight container for up to 4 weeks.

||||||||||||||||||||||||||||||||||||||||

Makes about 1 pound

GF, NF, SFO

Soy-Free Option: Use soy-free butter to make this soy-free.

MISSISSIPPI MUD PIE

Mississippi Mud Pie has many variations, but the chocolate stays consistent. This pie has as much chocolate as possible, starting with a chocolate cookie crust and ending with Cinnamon-Caramel Chocolate Crunch (page 117) pieces. The mousse-like chocolate filling is rich and decadent. To make this pie gluten-free, use a gluten-free chocolate cookie crust.

> 1 (9-inch) Chocolate Cookie or Graham Cracker Crust (page 88), baked and chilled
>
> **Mousse Pudding**
> 1 1/4 cups soymilk or Homemade Almond Milk (page 15), divided
> 2 tablespoons unsweetened Dutch-process cocoa powder
> 2 teaspoons instant coffee
> 1/8 teaspoon sea salt
> 3 tablespoons arrowroot or cornstarch
> 1 1/3 cups nondairy semisweet chocolate chips
> 1/2 teaspoon pure vanilla extract
> 1/3 cup aquafaba
> 1/4 cup granulated organic sugar
> 1/4 teaspoon cream of tartar
> Sweet Whipped Topping (page 88)
> Cinnamon-Caramel Chocolate Crunch (page 117), optional

1. Crust: Prepare the crust according to the recipe and refrigerate to chill before proceeding with the recipe. Combine 1 cup of the milk, cocoa, coffee, and salt in a medium saucepan over medium heat. Combine the remaining 1/4 cup milk and the arrowroot or cornstarch in a small bowl and set aside. Bring the milk to a boil, stir the starch slurry, slowly add it to the mixture using a spatula, and remove the mixture from the heat as soon as it thickens. Add the chocolate chips and vanilla and stir gently until the chocolate melts. Set aside to cool slightly.

2. Pudding: Add the aquafaba, sugar, and cream of tartar to the bowl of a stand mixer and whisk for 10 seconds with a whisk. Attach the balloon whip and whip for 5 minutes on medium-low speed. Increase the speed to medium-high and continue to whip until stiff peaks (page 5) form, about 8 more minutes.

3. Fold a large scoop of the meringue into the warm chocolate base until well incorporated. Fold in another large scoop. Fold in another large scoop, but begin to take care to not deflate any more of the meringue. Continue adding meringue until it is all used. Transfer the mousse to the pie crust. Chill in the refrigerator to firm up, about 4 hours.

4. Serve the pie garnished with Sweet Whipped Topping and Cinnamon-Caramel Chocolate Crunch.

Makes 1 (9-inch) pie

GFO, NF, SF

GRAHAM CRACKER CRUST

Make sure to use fresh graham crackers, not stale ones. This is probably the easiest crust to make and will become crisp upon cooling. You can even swap out any hard cookies you have on hand in place of the graham crackers. Use gluten-free graham crackers for a gluten-free version. Grind your crackers either in the food processor or crush them inside a bag with a rolling pin.

> 1 1/2 cups finely ground graham cracker crumbs (9 to 10 whole crackers)
> 1/4 cup granulated organic sugar
> 1/3 cup Butter (page 10) or store-bought nondairy butter, melted

1. Preheat the oven to 350°F. Combine the graham cracker crumbs, sugar, and butter in a medium bowl. Mix well to combine. Press the moistened crumbs into a lightly greased 9-inch pie plate, pressing well all along the sides and bottom. Press the crumbs into the sides first, then use the back of a measuring cup to help press the crumbs on the bottom evenly. Place the pie crust in the refrigerator for 15 minutes.

2. Bake the crust until it is golden, about 8 minutes. Chill completely before using.

Makes 1 (9-inch) crust

GFO, NF, SFO

Soy-Free Option: Use soy-free butter to make this soy-free.

Chocolate Cookie Crust: Use 18 whole chocolate sandwich cookies instead of the graham crackers. Remove and discard the cream filling before grinding the cookies.

SWEET WHIPPED TOPPING

This is my version of whipped cream that you can use to top ice cream sundaes, pies, and cakes. The topping is just rich enough to feel substantial without weighing you down. Whipping the aquafaba to stiff peaks (page 5) and stabilizing it with Glucose Syrup and coconut oil makes this topping just right. It's also ready quickly, as long as you have the aquafaba reduced beforehand. Prepare this topping in a cool kitchen since warmth and humidity can break the meringue once the oil is added. Add this topping to desserts right before serving, as it does break down over time.

> 1/4 cup cold Reduced Aquafaba (page 3)
> 3 tablespoons Glucose Syrup (page 80) or light corn syrup
> 1/4 teaspoon cream of tartar
> 2 tablespoons granulated organic sugar
> 1 tablespoon refined coconut oil, just melted and at room temperature
> 1/2 teaspoon pure vanilla extract

1. Add the reduced aquafaba, glucose syrup, and cream of tartar to the bowl of a stand mixer. Using the balloon whip attachment, whip the mixture on medium-low speed to reach soft peaks (page 5), about 5 minutes.

2. Increase the speed to medium-high and continue to whip until firm peaks (page 5) are reached, about 5 more minutes.

3. Add the sugar 1 tablespoon at a time over the course of 1 minute. Whip until the foam reaches stiff peaks (page 5), about 3 to 5 more minutes. Taste and adjust for sweetness. Add more sugar, if needed, but whip a minute more to dissolve it.

4. Add the room temperature oil in a slow, steady stream (or the foam will deflate too much). Add the vanilla in the same way. The foam will deflate considerably into a rich, thick topping. Transfer to an airtight container and store in the refrigerator for 2 to 4 hours. The topping will begin to deflate after that time.

||||||||||||||||||||||||||||||||||||||||||||
Makes about 6 servings

GF, NF, SF

LEMON MERINGUE PIE

||||||||||||||||||||||||||||||||||||||||||||||||||||||||||||||||||||||||||||||||||||||||||||||||||||

Katrina Stuart of Plantified.com is another innovator in the aquafaba kitchen. She has developed mousse recipes, cheesecake recipes, and, of course, her own version of lemon meringue pie. It is worthwhile to check out her creations. The meringue on my version of this pie will stay tall and proud until you devour it, so long as you don't rewhip the agar (see page 166). Spread the meringue onto the pie with a spatula and make peaks in it with the tip of the spatula but do not pipe it. Once the agar starts to set, piping will disturb the agar lattice and your meringue will deflate. Make this pie gluten-free by using a gluten-free crust.

Lemon Curd Filling
1 1/3 cups water, divided
1/4 cup arrowroot or cornstarch
1 teaspoon agar powder
1 cup fresh lemon juice
1/3 cup raw cashew pieces, soaked overnight
Pinch turmeric
1 1/4 cups granulated organic sugar
1 tablespoon nondairy butter (use soy-free vegan butter to make soy-free)
1 (9-inch) Traditional Pie Crust (page 92) or Graham Cracker Crust (page 88), prebaked

Meringue
3/4 cup aquafaba
3/4 teaspoon cream of tartar, divided
1 1/4 cups granulated organic sugar, divided
1/2 cup water
1 teaspoon agar powder

1. See the Candy Making section (page 74) before preparing the recipe.

2. **Filling:** Measure out 1 1/3 cup water and combine 1/2 cup of it with the arrowroot or cornstarch to form a slurry; set aside. Combine the remaining 5/6 cup water and the agar in a medium saucepan and set aside for 3 minutes to soften. Blend the lemon juice, cashews, and turmeric in a blender until very smooth, scraping the sides as needed; set aside.

3. Add the sugar to the agar mixture and bring it to a boil over medium heat, stirring occasionally. Cook the mixture for 5 minutes to completely dissolve the agar. Add the lemon mixture and return to a simmer. Add the starch slurry and return to a simmer. Gently stir the mixture and cook for 30 seconds. Remove the filling from the heat and stir in the butter. Set the filling aside to mostly cool before adding it to the crust.

4. **Meringue:** Add the aquafaba and 1/2 teaspoon of the cream of tartar to the bowl of a stand mixer. Using a whisk, whip the aquafaba for 10 seconds. Using a balloon whip attachment, whip the aquafaba on medium power for 5 minutes. Increase the speed to medium-high and continue to whip for another 5 minutes, or until the aquafaba can hold firm peaks (page 5). Add 1/4 cup of the sugar, 1 tablespoon at a time, over the span of a minute and continue to whip until the meringue can hold stiff peaks (page 5).

5. Add the 1/2 cup water and agar to a heavy-bottomed medium saucepan. Set aside to soften for 3 minutes. Add the remaining 1/4 teaspoon cream of tartar and the remaining 1 cup sugar to the middle of the water. Bring the mixture to a boil, stirring constantly to melt the sugar (this will take a few minutes), over medium-high heat. Reduce the heat to medium and cover the saucepan with a tight-fitting lid. Cook for 3 minutes. Remove the lid, wash the sides of the pan with water and attach a candy thermometer; do not stir again. Cook the syrup until it reaches 260°F (hard-ball stage). Turn off the heat and allow the sugar syrup to cool for a few minutes, or until it is no longer bubbling; do not move or jiggle the pan until then.

6. Once the meringue is ready, slow the machine and add the sugar syrup slowly in a steady stream, trying not to touch the sides of the bowl or the whisk. Once all the syrup has been added, increase the speed to medium-high and whip for 4 minutes until the meringue is much cooler.

7. Spread the meringue on the still-warm filling, spreading it to the edges of the crust to reduce shrinking. Cool the pie completely overnight before browning the meringue with a pastry torch or under a broiler. If using a broiler, turn the pie every 10 seconds until browned, 1 to 2 minutes, to evenly brown the meringue.

||||||||||||||||||||||||||||||||||||

Makes 1 (9-inch) pie

GFO, NFO, SFO

Nut-Free Option: Combine 1/2 cup water and 1/4 cup cornstarch and set aside. Combine the agar, lemon juice, turmeric, sugar, and 1 1/2 cups canned coconut cream (not canned coconut milk) in a medium saucepan and whisk well to combine. Bring the mixture to a boil over medium heat, reduce to a simmer, and cook, stirring, until the agar dissolves and the mixture reaches 195°F, 8 to 10 minutes. Continue with the recipe as directed in Step 2 by adding the starch slurry.

TRADITIONAL PIE CRUST

This recipe makes a double-crusted pie (or two single-crust pies). If you have a pastry cutter, you can make this in one bowl, but the advantage of mixing the butter, flour, and milk in a separate bowl is that you can feel how the dough is absorbing the liquid. The dough needs a few minutes to absorb the proper amount of moisture, and that is harder to gauge in a machine. It also prevents overmixing as developing the gluten makes the crust tough.

> 1/2 cup Butter (page 10) or store-bought nondairy butter
> 1/2 cup plus 2 tablespoons plain unsweetened nondairy milk
> 1 tablespoon apple cider vinegar
> 2 1/2 cups unbleached all-purpose flour
> 1 teaspoon to 1 tablespoon granulated organic sugar
> 1 teaspoon sea salt

1. Cut the butter into 1/2-inch cubes and place them in the freezer for 5 to 10 minutes. Combine the milk and vinegar in a separate container and place it in the freezer for 5 to 10 minutes.

2. Combine the flour, sugar (use 1 tablespoon for sweet pies), and salt in a food processor. Pulse to combine well. Add the chilled butter and pulse to chop into coarse crumbs. Transfer the flour mixture to a medium bowl.

3. Add half the milk mixture to the flour mixture and, using a spatula, stir to mix well. The flour will take a minute or two to absorb all the liquid. Add more milk and stir again. Add only enough milk to create a dough that will stick together when squeezed; however, it is best to have a dough that is moist than dry (otherwise, it will be difficult to roll and the crust will crack). Form the dough into two disks, but do not knead as kneading will form lots of gluten threads and make the crust tough. Wrap the dough in wax paper and chill in the refrigerator for at least 30 minutes. If chilled for longer than 1 hour, set at room temperature for 10 minutes to soften up.

4. Preheat the oven to 400°F. Roll the dough out into a 13-inch circle on a lightly floured surface and transfer it to a 9-inch pie plate. Crimp the edges by tucking under the excess dough and using your fingers to create pleats.

5. Place a piece of parchment paper on the dough and add 1 1/2 pounds of dried beans to the pie plate, leveling out the beans. Bake the crust until the edges are turning golden brown, about 12 minutes (this is par-baking). Remove the parchment with the beans and return the pie crust to the oven. Bake until the crust is golden brown throughout, about 10 more minutes (this is prebaking). Allow the crust to cool completely before using.

||||||||||||||||||||||||||||||||||||||
Makes 2 (9-inch) crusts

NF, SFO

Soy-Free Option: Use soy-free vegan butter.

COCONUT-KEY LIME CREAM PIE

Traditionally, key lime pie is made with sweetened condensed milk and, depending on the recipe, it can boast a creamy citrus filling. This one is made with coconut cream instead, because it just makes sense: put the lime in the coconut, as the saying has it. Make this pie gluten-free by using a gluten-free crust.

1/4 cup aquafaba
1 1/2 teaspoons agar powder
1/2 cup granulated organic sugar
1/2 cup fresh key lime or lime juice, divided
1 (14-ounce) can coconut cream (not canned coconut milk)
1 teaspoon pure vanilla extract
Zest of 1 lime
1 Graham Cracker Crust (page 88)
Sweet Whipped Topping (page 88), optional

1. Combine the aquafaba and agar in a small saucepan, mix well, and set aside for 3 minutes. Add the sugar and 1/4 cup of the lime juice, bring to a boil over medium-high heat, and reduce to a simmer over medium heat. Cook, stirring, until the agar comes up to 195°F, about 5 minutes. Immediately add the sugar syrup to the bowl of a stand mixer fitted with a balloon whip attachment. Whisk on medium-high until the syrup flows in thick ribbons, about 7 minutes.

2. Reduce the mixer speed to medium and slowly add the remaining 1/4 cup lime juice. When well incorporated, add the coconut cream 1 heaping tablespoon at a time. Incorporate and emulsify each portion before adding more. Add the vanilla and continue to mix until very smooth. Transfer the filling to the prepared crust. Garnish the pie with the zest and chill in the refrigerator overnight to firm up. Serve with the whipped topping, if desired.

Makes 1 (9-inch) pie

GFO, NF, SF

CHOCOLATE ICE CREAM

Cocoa powder adds additional fat to an ice cream, but I made sure that this soy version of ice cream would be just as great without the chocolate, so feel free to omit it and make this into Vanilla Ice Cream, Berry Swirl Ice Cream, or Caramel-Praline Ice Cream. Although this ice cream hardens in the freezer, the ice cream will soften just perfectly after a few minutes out of the freezer because of the addition of glucose syrup. If you'd like to omit the glucose syrup, add three more tablespoons sugar to the base.

Cream Base
1 tablespoon arrowroot or cornstarch
3 cups plain unsweetened soymilk, divided
1/2 cup lightly packed mashed firm tofu, rinsed before mashing
1 teaspoon psyllium husk powder
5 tablespoons nondairy butter, melted
1/2 cup unsweetened Dutch-process cocoa powder
1/2 cup plus 1 tablespoon granulated organic sugar
2 tablespoons Glucose Syrup (page 80) or light corn syrup
1/4 teaspoon sea salt
1 teaspoon pure vanilla extract

Meringue
1/3 cup aquafaba
1/4 teaspoon cream of tartar
1/4 cup granulated organic sugar
1/4 cup Cinnamon-Caramel Chocolate Crunch (page 117), optional

1. **Cream Base:** Combine the starch with 1/4 cup of the milk to form a slurry and set aside. Combine 1 cup of the milk, the tofu, and psyllium husk powder in a blender. Blend until very smooth. With the blender running, add the melted butter in a slow, steady stream to emulsify.

2. Transfer the tofu mixture to a medium saucepan. Add the remaining 1 3/4 cups milk, cocoa, sugar, glucose syrup, and salt to the saucepan. Stir well with a whisk and bring to a boil over medium heat, making sure all the cocoa and sugar are dissolved. Add the starch slurry and reduce to a simmer, gently stirring until slightly thickened. Remove the cream base from the heat and stir in the vanilla. Transfer the cream base to a medium bowl and set aside to cool to room temperature.

3. **Meringue:** Add the aquafaba and cream of tartar to the bowl of a stand mixer. Using a whisk, whip the aquafaba for 10 seconds. Using a balloon whip attachment, whip the aquafaba on medium speed for 5 minutes. Increase the speed to medium-high and continue to whip for another 5 to 8 minutes, or until the aquafaba can hold stiff peaks (page 5) and is climbing the side of the bowl. Add the sugar, 1 tablespoon at a time, over the course of 3 minutes and continue to whip until the sugar has dissolved, about 3 more minutes.

4. Add a large scoop of the meringue to the cooled cream base and mix well. Add the rest of the meringue to the tempered cream base and fold to mix thoroughly. Chill in the refrigerator until completely cold, about 8 hours.

5. It is normal if the cream base has separated somewhat overnight. Gently mix the chilled base and, using an ice cream machine, churn the cream as instructed by the manufacturer. Stir in the crunch pieces about 3 minutes before the ice cream is well churned. Enjoy it as soft serve immediately or transfer it to an airtight, freezer-safe container and freeze. Allow the ice cream to soften 10 to 20 minutes before serving if completely frozen.

||||||||||||||||||||||||||||||||||||
Makes about 1 quart

GF, NF

Variations: Make this recipe into any of the other ice creams in this book by omitting the cocoa powder and reducing the sugar in the base by 1/4 cup. Then follow the instructions below.

- **Vanilla Ice Cream:** Increase the vanilla to 2 teaspoons.
- **Berry Swirl Ice Cream:** Stir 3 to 4 tablespoons of berry purée (page 99) into the finished ice cream.
- **Caramel-Praline Ice Cream:** Add in 3 to 4 tablespoons caramel sauce (page 101) and 1/2 cup chopped pecan pralines (page 101) during the last minute of churning.

BERRY SWIRL-COCONUT ICE CREAM

Ice crystals form in ice cream each time it is thawed and refrozen, so I recommend storing your homemade ice cream in smaller containers. This makes it easier to serve and prevents additional crystals from forming. Although this ice cream hardens in the freezer, remember that it will soften after a few minutes out of the freezer because of the addition of Glucose Syrup. If you prefer to omit the glucose syrup, add six more tablespoons of sugar to the base.

Cream Base
2 (13.5-ounce) cans full-fat coconut milk, refrigerated 1 hour and divided
1 tablespoon arrowroot or cornstarch
1/4 cup Glucose Syrup (page 80) or light corn syrup
2 tablespoons granulated organic sugar
1 teaspoon psyllium husk powder
1/8 teaspoon sea salt
2 teaspoons pure vanilla extract

Meringue
1/2 cup aquafaba
1/4 teaspoon cream of tartar
1/4 cup granulated organic sugar

Berry Purée
1 (10-ounce) bag frozen berries (about 2 1/2 cups)
2 tablespoons granulated organic sugar

1. Cream Base: Scoop out the coconut cream from 1 can of coconut milk and add it to a medium saucepan. Discard 1/3 cup of the liquid from the can. Combine about 1/4 cup of the remaining liquid with the arrowroot or cornstarch to form a slurry and set aside. Add the rest of the can's contents and the second can of coconut milk to the pan along with the glucose syrup, sugar, psyllium husk powder, and salt. Bring the mixture to a simmer over medium heat and cook until thickened, about 1 minute, stirring often with a whisk. Add the starch slurry and return to a simmer to thicken, stirring gently. Remove the cream base from the heat, stir in the vanilla, transfer to a large bowl, and cool to room temperature before adding the meringue.

2. Meringue: Add the aquafaba and cream of tartar to the bowl of a stand mixer. Using a whisk, whip the aquafaba for 10 seconds. Using a balloon whip attachment, whip the aquafaba on medium speed for 5 minutes. Increase the speed to medium-high and continue to whip for another 5 to 8 minutes, or until the aquafaba can hold stiff peaks (page 5) and is climbing the side of the bowl. Add the sugar, 1 tablespoon at a time, over the course of 3 minutes and continue to whip until the sugar has dissolved, about 3 more minutes.

3. Add a large scoop of the meringue to the cooled cream base and mix well. Add the rest of the meringue to the tempered cream base and fold to mix thoroughly. Chill in the refrigerator until completely cold, about 8 hours.

4. Berry Purée: Combine the berries and the sugar in a medium saucepan over medium heat. Cover and cook until the berries break down, 10 to 13 minutes, stirring once. (If using strawberries, blend the berries to break them down.) Transfer the berries to a fine-mesh strainer set over a bowl. Sieve the berries through to remove all the seeds; you should have 1 cup of purée. Return the purée to the pan and cook over medium heat until reduced by half, 13 to 16 minutes, stirring more toward the end of the cooking. Chill completely before using.

5. Freeze the ice cream in an ice cream machine as directed by the manufacturer. Using a large spoon, stir in 3 to 4 tablespoons of berry purée, leaving streaks of the purée in the ice cream. Enjoy it as soft serve immediately or transfer it to an airtight, freezer-safe container and freeze. Allow the ice cream to soften for 10 to 20 minutes before serving if completely frozen.

||||||||||||||||||||||||||||||||||||||||||||
Makes about 1 quart

GF, NF, SF

Variations: Make this recipe into any of the other ice creams in this book by omitting the berry purée and following the instructions below.

- **Vanilla Ice Cream:** Scrape out the insides of a vanilla pod and add it to the pan with the coconut cream. Add the pod to the pan also, but remove it before chilling the base.
- **Caramel-Praline Ice Cream:** Add in 3 to 4 tablespoons caramel sauce (page 101) and 1/2 cup chopped pecan pralines (page 101) during the last minute of churning.
- **Chocolate Ice Cream:** Add 1/2 cup unsweetened Dutch-process cocoa powder and 1/4 cup sugar to the base before cooking it.

CARAMEL-PRALINE CASHEW ICE CREAM

All three ice cream bases are creamy and rich. Although the glucose syrup softens the ice cream perfectly even when completely frozen, if you'd like to omit it, add three more tablespoons sugar to the base.

Cream Base
2 3/4 cups nondairy milk, divided
1 tablespoon arrowroot or cornstarch
1 1/2 cups raw cashew pieces
1 teaspoon psyllium husk powder
1/8 teaspoon sea salt
5 tablespoons granulated organic sugar
2 tablespoons Glucose Syrup (page 80) or
    light corn syrup

1 teaspoon pure vanilla extract

Meringue
1/2 cup aquafaba
1/4 teaspoon cream of tartar
1/4 cup granulated organic sugar
3 to 4 tablespoons Caramel Sauce (recipe follows)
2/3 cup Pecan Pralines, chopped (recipe follows)

1. Cream Base: Combine 1/4 cup of the milk with the arrowroot or cornstarch to form a slurry and set aside. Combine the cashews and 1 1/2 cups of the milk in a blender. Blend until very smooth and not grainy (see Nuts, blending, page 166). Add the psyllium husk powder, salt, and the remaining 1 cup milk. Blend again until smooth. Transfer the mixture, along with the sugar and glucose syrup, to a medium saucepan and cook over medium heat until the mixture comes to a simmer, stirring often with a whisk. When it comes to a simmer, add the starch slurry, stirring gently until it returns to a simmer. Transfer the cream base to a large bowl and cool to room temperature. Once cool, stir in the vanilla.

2. Meringue: Add the aquafaba and cream of tartar to a stand mixer. Using a whisk, whip the aquafaba for 10 seconds. Using a balloon whip attachment, whip the aquafaba on medium speed for 5 minutes. Increase the speed to medium-high and continue to whip for another 5 to 8 minutes, or until the aquafaba can hold stiff peaks (page 5) and is climbing the side of the bowl. Add the sugar, 1 tablespoon at a time, over the course of 3 minutes and continue to whip until the sugar has dissolved, about 3 more minutes.

3. Add about one-fourth of the meringue to the cooled cream base and mix. Once the meringue is well incorporated, add the rest of the meringue and fold gently until the mixture is homogeneous. Chill the base in the refrigerator overnight. Gently mix the chilled base and, using an ice cream machine, churn the cream as instructed by the manufacturer. During the last minute of churning, stream in the caramel sauce and add the pecan pralines. Eat as soft serve immediately, or transfer to a freezer-safe container and freeze 3 to 4 hours until firm. If frozen overnight, allow the ice cream to thaw for 20 to 30 minutes before serving.

Makes about 1 quart

GF, SF

Variations: Make into any of the other ice creams in this book by omitting the caramel sauce and pecan pralines and following the instructions below.

- **Vanilla Ice Cream:** Increase the vanilla to 2 teaspoons.
- **Berry Swirl Ice Cream:** Stir 3 to 4 tablespoons berry purée (page 99) into the finished ice cream.

- **Chocolate Ice Cream:** Add 1/2 cup unsweetened Dutch-process cocoa powder and 1/4 cup sugar to the base before cooking it.
- **Fudge Brownie Ice Cream:** During the last 2 minutes of churning in the ice cream machine, add 1 cup chopped Chewy Fudge Brownies (page 131) to the machine.

CARAMEL SAUCE

1/2 cup packed Light Brown Sugar (page 23) or store-bought light brown sugar
1/4 cup nondairy milk
2 tablespoons nondairy butter (or soy-free vegan butter)
1 tablespoon Glucose Syrup (page 80) or light corn syrup
1/2 teaspoon pure vanilla extract

See the Candy Making section (page 74) before preparing the recipe. Combine the brown sugar, milk, butter, and glucose syrup in a small saucepan over medium heat. Bring to a boil, stirring to dissolve all the sugar. Add a tight-fitting lid and cook for 3 minutes to wash the sides of any stray sugar. Attach a candy thermometer and cook the syrup, without stirring, until it reaches 230°F (for use in ice cream). If using the caramel sauce for macarons, cook the syrup to 242°F. Gently remove the sauce from the heat and allow it to cool to room temperature without disturbing it. Stir in the vanilla and transfer the sauce to an airtight container. Store in the refrigerator for up to 2 weeks. Stir the sauce before using as an ice cream addition.

Makes about 3/4 cup

GF, NF, SFO

PECAN PRALINES

1 cup whole raw pecans
1/4 cup packed Light Brown Sugar (page 23) or store-bought light brown sugar
2 tablespoons plain unsweetened nondairy milk
1 tablespoon nondairy butter (use soy-free for a soy-free option)
1/2 teaspoon pure vanilla extract

Preheat the oven to 350°F. Combine the pecans, brown sugar, milk, and butter in a cake pan. Bake for 2 minutes to melt the butter. Stir well. Bake for 10 more minutes and stir. Bake for an additional 8 to 10 minutes, or until the sauce is thick and the nuts smell toasted. Do not burn. Transfer the pecans to a silicone mat or piece of parchment paper and allow them to cool completely. Once the pralines are hardened, store them in an airtight container for up to 4 weeks.

Makes about 1 cup

GF, SFO

SWEETS FROM THE OVEN

This chapter contains recipes that require oven heat to prepare: cookies, cakes, and even a delectable bread pudding. In addition, I've included supplemental recipes that will round out your creations, such as buttercream and royal icing. There is even a cookie recipe from my childhood, Dutch Butter Cookies, which I remember selling during the holidays for fundraising.

MERINGUE COOKIES

Goose Wohlt brought us the meringue cookie back in 2015 and we were both amazed and excited. This is the very first recipe that is made by newbie aquafaba explorers, and it is still wonderful when someone new posts their first meringue cookie on the Facebook group Vegan Meringue – Hits and Misses! If this is your first experience with this airy and crisp cookie, snap a pic and post for everyone to celebrate with you.

1/3 cup granulated organic sugar
1/2 cup aquafaba
1/4 teaspoon cream of tartar

1. If your sugar is not fine granules, grind it for 1 minute in a food processor. Prepare a baking sheet with parchment paper or a silicone mat (the meringue will deflate if baked directly on a baking sheet). Preheat the oven to 195°F.

2. Add the aquafaba and cream of tartar to the bowl of a stand mixer. Use a whisk or the balloon whip attachment to hand-whip the aquafaba for 10 seconds. Add the balloon whip to the machine or use a hand mixer to whip the aquafaba for 4 minutes at medium-low speed. Increase the speed to medium-high and continue to whip for 5 to 6 minutes or until the meringue forms firm peaks (page 5).

3. Continue to whip on medium-high speed and add the sugar, 1 tablespoon at a time, over the course of 1 minute. Continue to beat for another 3 to 4 minutes, or until the meringue forms stiff peaks (page 5). Alternatively, you can use a large bowl and a hand mixer.

4. Spoon or pipe the meringue onto the prepared baking sheet, about 2 inches apart. Bake the cookies for 1 1/2 hours, turn off the oven, leave the cookies inside the oven, and allow them to cool completely. Once cooled, immediately transfer them to an airtight container. If left out long enough, the cookies will absorb the moisture in the air and become tacky and then dissolve. If your cookies become tacky or begin to absorb moisture, dehydrate again in the oven at 195°F until crisp. You can adjust how crisp you like the cookies by leaving them exposed to the air until they are the texture you like.

Makes 20 to 40 cookies, depending on the size of the cookies

GF, NF, SF

Chocolate Meringue Cookies: After the meringue is whipped, sift in 2 teaspoons unsweetened Dutch-process cocoa powder. Fold just to mix most of the cocoa into the meringue, but don't fold too much or the meringue might deflate.

Swirl-Colored Cookies: To add a swirl to these cookies (as pictured opposite), prepare the empty piping bag by drawing three or four vertical food-coloring lines inside the bag, using a toothpick or the tip of a butter knife. Draw your lines from down near the tip upward toward the middle of the bag. Use any color of natural food coloring. Once you have prepared the bag, proceed with Step 4.

Macaron Primer: Tips, Techniques, and Troubleshooting

Macarons are by far the most challenging cookies to make—perfectly. Through my trials and tribulations, I can tell you that even if your macarons do not have the perfect feet, aren't smooth and shiny, or have some hollow sections in the middle, they are still very tasty little cookies to enjoy. Perfection is relative, anyway, so enjoy the process of baking these tender, crisp little bites of deliciousness. With practice, even macarons can be perfected.

A showstopper aquafaba creation, macarons were among the first things that folks started making when aquafaba hit the web. Charis Mitchell of FloralFrosting.blogspot.com led that parade when she posted recipes and a video about the process. She demystified the elusive macaronage, which is the way to properly deflate and mix the batter, for those of us who had previously never even dreamed of making vegan macarons.

There are three kinds of meringues and, therefore, three kinds of macarons, each named after the method that is used to make the meringues:

- **French meringue** is first whipped then strengthened with the addition of granulated sugar.

- **Italian meringue** is first whipped and then strengthened with the addition of hot sugar syrup.

- **Swiss meringue** is made by cooking aquafaba and sugar together and then whipping it into a meringue.

How to Make French Meringue

By far, the easiest method is the French meringue; therefore, the macarons in this book will use the French method to make the cookies. Adding granulated sugar to the meringue reinforces the structure of the foam and therefore is not optional to use. Making sugar-free meringue is a science all to itself and is best left to another book.

There are three basic components of a macaron: the **nut flour** (there is an optional nut-free macaron in this section), **the meringue**, and the **macaronage** (or how the flour mixture is folded with the meringue). Macarons are made when all three components are brought together in harmony.

Measurements. The measurement of the dry ingredients by **weight** is critical because the flour, granulated sugar, and confectioners' sugar must be in perfect balance; otherwise, your macarons will develop some defect. For this reason, I have given the measurement of weights for the granulated sugar, confectioners' sugar, and almond meal in both ounces (by weight, not volume) and grams. Measuring by volume can be highly varied, leading to burst macarons, unevenly baked macarons, or macarons that don't produce enough steam to rise properly.

Nut or Seed Flour. The flour must be ground very finely. Commercially purchased flour is your best bet; use very finely ground blanched almond flour. If making your own flour, see page 111.

Meringue. The meringue for macarons must be whipped to stiff peaks (page 5). This means that when you dip the beater into the meringue and lift it straight up, the peak that the meringue forms does not flop over at all but holds its peak without wavering. Some good indicators of a stiff peak while you are whipping is that the meringue is glossy, pure white, and begins climbing the sides of your bowl. When in doubt, whip longer. Unlike egg whites, aquafaba will not overwhip and can be whipped for an hour without any adverse effects.

Macaronage. This is the most difficult part to master and it will take some experience to get a good feel for how your folding is turning out. Overfolding will render a watery mess and underfolding will make cookies that are granular looking and have concentric circles in them from the piping.

To fold your macarons, stir around the outside of the bowl using the flat part of a large silicone spatula, almost like you are moving everything toward the middle. Make sure the spatula's flat part is hugging the bowl and that you aren't using the edge like a knife, cutting through the meringue. Then, again using the flat of your spatula, move the spatula against the side of the bowl upward, in a wavy, wiggly motion. This presses out air. Turn the bowl a bit and repeat. Every three or four folds, stir around the side of the bowl, angling the spatula to hug the sides and bottom of the bowl, making sure to mix in any almond flour on the bottom of the bowl.

Repeat this procedure until your batter flows like lava. Scoop up some batter and allow it to fall back to the bowl. If it drops from your spatula in a big plop or doesn't drop for a while, continue to fold. Check often as you continue to fold because you can't unfold. If your batter flows off like pancake batter, it is overfolded. Keep in mind that how the batter falls from your spatula into the bowl will be about how it pipes onto the baking sheet. It should not keep any indentations in the cookie, but it must hold its shape into a disk; it is a very fine line that experience will help you learn to judge. Also important to note is that the act of piping will continue to deflate your batter ever so slightly. As I once read, if your arm doesn't hurt by the end of the macaronage, you didn't macaron enough.

Now that you've made your batter, it's time to create the cookie by piping the batter onto a parchment paper using a piping bag.

Piping: Use a piping bag with a 1/2-inch tip (Wilton #2A). Pipe the batter onto parchment paper (secure the corners of the paper by dotting the corners under the paper with some batter) or silicone mats. Place your piping bag perpendicular to the baking sheet, about 1/2 inch above the sheet, and pipe straight down. If you have tips on the ends of the macarons, but you have folded just right, the next step will remove them.

Pipe the same size circles consistently for even baking. For small macarons, pipe 1-inch circles and for large macarons, pipe 1 1/2-inch circles. It is easiest to count while you pipe. I pipe for a 2-second count for small macarons and a 3-second count for the large ones. This actually makes for more evenly sized shells. Pipe them about 2 inches apart. Too many cookies per tray can lead to uneven baking and cookies that fail in some way.

Baking: I recommend silicone mats for even baking; never pipe onto a bare baking sheet. If your baking pan is very thin, double up and place another pan under it; this will ensure that your pan evenly distributes heat to all the cookies.

One of the causes of hollow cookies is the trapped air bubbles in the batter. Once you've piped the batter, drop your pan onto the counter or a sturdy table from a height of 2 to 3 feet. Drop them about 5 to 10 times to release any large air bubbles. If you macaroned correctly, the cookies will even out with no visible concentric circles. If there are tiny peaks left in the macaron, I wouldn't worry about them. Some folks say to dampen your finger and even it out, but every time I've done that the macaron failed in one way or another, so I just leave them be.

Dry your macarons under a fan or in a dehydrator (with no heat), or just air-dry them until they are dry to the touch. This is important for the development of the feet. Be aware that humidity and hot weather can interfere with baking macarons; it can lead to hollow macarons, exploded macarons, or stuck macarons.

Bake one sheet of macarons at a time. Preheat the oven and use an oven thermometer—if the temperature of the oven is too hot, the macarons will burst or melt instead of bake (the meringue will completely break down). On the other hand, if your oven is too cold, the macarons won't bake through and will stick to the mat. Because of the low oven temperature that is required, there is very little wiggle room for variations in temperature. An oven thermometer reduces a lot of stress and is essential for making successful macarons.

Cool the macarons on the baking sheet before removing them. If your shells do not come off the mat easily and you know the temperature of your oven, try increasing the time of baking by 5 minutes for subsequent batches. Also, watch the temperature in the oven as it can increase when baking for a prolonged time. Store the macarons in an airtight container at room temperature.

Once the macarons are filled, store them in the refrigerator in an airtight container for a few days.

If your macaron shells are too crisp, leave them open to the air to absorb some moisture and soften; a few hours should be enough. Once filled, the macarons will absorb moisture form the filling and soften more, so keep that in mind.

Start with the Basic Macaron Shells (page 110), which are made without any coloring or flavoring. "Plain" macarons taste like almonds, so they are delicious in their own right and making them will give you some experience before you attempt the more complex ones. Typically, it is the filling that determines the flavor of the macarons and the shells are just colored to give the eye the idea of what the flavor is. For instance, red shells might indicate that the macaron's flavor is strawberry or raspberry, but even if it is only the filling that is flavored (see the Berry Buttercream [page 118] from the Strawberry Shortcake Macaron), the entire cookie will taste of berries, whether or not the shell is actually flavored.

Troubleshooting Chart

- The aquafaba doesn't whip. Added oil, food coloring, or other flavoring before macaronage can prevent aquafaba from whipping properly. Wait to add anything—besides sugar and cream of tartar—to the aquafaba until the macaronage stage.

- The aquafaba deflated too fast after adding the almond meal mixture. This means that the aquafaba was not whipped to stiff peaks. Review Whipping Aquafaba (page 5).

- The shells are too bumpy. This means that the almond flour was not incorporated properly, the almond meal is too coarse or not sifted properly. Process the almond flour longer and sift it using a very fine mesh strainer.

- The shells are too stiff, with concentric circles, after piping. The batter is too stiff. Macaronage a few more turns and test for proper consistency. If you notice the concentric circles after piping only a few shells, squeeze out all the batter back to the bowl and return to the piping bag. The squeezing of the piping bag will have deflated more of the batter.

- The shells flow into each other or do not hold their shape. This means the batter has been over-macaroned. Macaronage a few less turns and test for proper consistency.

- The shells have no feet. This means there is not enough sugar in the batter; measure more accurately. It could also mean that the baking sheet is too thin; double up the sheets for more even heating. The oven temperature may be too low; check the temperature using an oven thermometer and increase the temperature (if needed) by 5 degrees, but do not exceed 240°F.

- No feet developed and the tops burst. This is caused by humidity or oven temperature. Make macarons on less humid days. Check the oven temperature using an oven thermometer and decrease the oven temperature by 5 or 10 degrees. Make sure to slam the baking sheet well to release any large air pockets. This problem could also be because the shells aren't dry enough before baking. If making nut-free macarons, make sure to dry the shells longer before baking. The problem could also be from over-macaroning.

- The macarons stick to the silicone mat. This can be caused by a dirty mat, an old mat, or by not baking the macarons long enough. Wash or replace your silicone mat. Increase the baking time by 5 minutes. Place the baking sheet in the freezer for 5 minutes if the macarons are fully cooked and are just sticking. Use an offset spatula to remove the shells. Oven temperature can also be the problem; check the oven temperature using an oven thermometer.

- The shells bake inconsistently and have angled feet. Uneven oven temperature is likely the cause. Rotate the baking sheet every 4 minutes for the first 12 minutes in the oven. Try baking the shells in different parts of the oven: the bottom third, the middle, and the top third. Other than that, there is not much you can do to change how your oven heats.

- The shells are hollow. This means the baking sheet was not slammed hard enough after piping. Slam your baking sheet well to remove any large air pockets in the batter. Humidity can also be the culprit.

- The shells slide off the feet. This means your baking sheet is too thin. Double up your baking sheet and use a silicone mat to evenly distribute heat. Don't crowd your sheets. Pipe no more than 20 large shells per tray. Give them room to cook.

BASIC MACARON SHELLS

These are the "plain" shells that are clean and crisp and are the perfect place to start when first making macarons. Once you are happy with how these turn out, you can tackle the other macarons in this book and even branch out and come up with your own flavors.

> 6 tablespoons aquafaba
> 3 ounces (85 grams) granulated organic sugar
> 1/4 teaspoon cream of tartar
> 3.35 ounces (95 grams) almond meal
> 3 ounces (85 grams) confectioners' sugar

1. Prepare two baking sheets with parchment paper or silicone mats and set aside. Add the aquafaba, granulated sugar, and cream of tartar to the bowl of a stand mixer. Use a whisk or the balloon whip attachment to hand-whip the aquafaba for 10 seconds. Add the balloon whip to the machine or use a hand mixer to whip the aquafaba for 4 minutes at medium-low speed. Increase the speed to medium-high and continue to whip until stiff peaks (page 5) form, about 10 to 14 minutes.

2. Add the almond meal and confectioners' sugar to the bowl of a food processor. Give the food processor 4 (3-second) pulses, scraping down the sides of the bowl between each pulse. Sift the mixture using a very fine mesh strainer. If the mixture doesn't pass through the sieve, the almonds are not ground finely enough.

3. Sift the mixture on top of the meringue and macaronage (page 107) the mixture until the batter flows like lava. Transfer the batter to a piping bag fitted with a 1/2-inch tip. Pipe 1 1/2-inch circles about 2 inches apart on the baking sheet. Bang the sheets on the counter 5 to 10 times to remove air pockets. Place the sheets in the open air to dry the batter, about 1 1/2 to 2 hours; the cookies should be dry to the touch. Preheat the oven to 230°F. Arrange the rack in the top third of the oven. Bake one sheet of cookies, placed on the top rack, for 35 to 40 minutes (30 to 35 minutes for small macarons). Transfer the baking sheet to a cooling rack until the cookies are completely cool.

4. Store the cookie shells in an airtight container until you are ready to fill and eat, up to 3 weeks.

Makes about 30 to 40 large shells

GF, SF

BASIC NUT-FREE MACARON SHELLS

Pepita seeds make the perfect replacement for almonds in macaron shells. In fact, they can be replaced on a one-to-one basis. Making your own pepita flour is easy, but it does have to be ground very finely (with care being taken not to turn it into butter).

> 1 1/2 cups raw pepitas (or 2 cups blanched almonds if making homemade nut flour)
> 6 tablespoons aquafaba
> 3 ounces (85 grams) granulated organic sugar
> 1/4 teaspoon cream of tartar
> 3 ounces (85 grams) confectioners' sugar
> 1 teaspoon vanilla bean powder

1. Make the pepita flour by adding the seeds to a food processor. Process for 20 seconds to break up the seeds. Continue processing the seeds by pulsing, about 50 pulses. Scrape the side of the bowl every 5 pulses. This will prevent the machine from overheating and the seeds from turning to butter.

2. Pass the pepita flour through a very fine mesh strainer. Any flour pieces that didn't pass through need to be processed again until the seeds are fine enough.

3. Prepare two baking sheets with parchment paper or silicone mats and set aside. Add the aquafaba, granulated sugar, and cream of tartar to the bowl of a stand mixer. Use a whisk or the balloon whip attachment to hand-whip the aquafaba for 10 seconds. Add the balloon whip to the machine or use a hand mixer to whip the aquafaba for 4 minutes at medium-low speed. Increase the speed to medium-high and continue to whip until the meringue reaches stiff peaks (page 5), about 10 to 14 minutes.

4. Measure out 3.35 ounces (95 grams) of the pepita flour. Add it and the confectioners' sugar to the bowl of a food processor. Give the food processor 4 (3-second) pulses, scraping down the side of the bowl between each pulse. Sift the mixture using a very fine mesh strainer.

5. Sift the mixture on top of the meringue and macaronage (page 107) the mixture until the batter flows like lava. Transfer the batter to a piping bag fitted with a 1/2-inch tip. Pipe 1 1/2-inch circles about 2 inches apart on the baking sheet. Bang the sheets on the counter 5 to 10 times to remove air pockets. Place the sheets in the open air to dry the batter, about 2 to 3 hours; the cookies should be dry to the touch. Preheat the oven to 230°F. Arrange the rack in the top third of the oven. Bake one sheet of cookies, placed on the top rack, for 35 to 40 minutes (30 to 35 minutes for small macarons). Transfer the baking sheet to a cooling rack until the cookies are completely cool.

6. Store the cookie shells in an airtight container until you are ready to fill and eat, up to 3 weeks.

Makes about 30 to 40 large shells

GF, NF, SF

STRAWBERRY SHORTCAKE MACARONS

These shells have a delightful berry flavor and pink color, if you plan on using a food coloring. There are natural food colorings available now, with red being made from hibiscus. Because of the added purée, these shells also use more almond meal. For the Strawberry Shortcake version, use strawberries in the purée. For a Raspberry Shortcake version, use raspberries.

Berry Macaron Shell
6 tablespoons aquafaba
3 ounces (85 grams) granulated organic sugar
1/4 teaspoon cream of tartar
1 teaspoon Berry Purée (page 99)
Few drops red food coloring, optional
3.9 ounces (110 grams) almond meal
3 ounces (85 grams) confectioners' sugar

Berry Buttercream
1/2 cup Swiss Buttercream (page 115), freshly made or rewhipped
2 tablespoons Berry Purée (page 99)
Red food coloring, optional

1. Shells: Prepare the shells as for Basic Macaron Shells (page 110), following the ingredient amounts listed here. Remove about 1/4 cup of the meringue and transfer it to a small bowl. Add the Berry Purée and food coloring (if using) to the small bowl and fold to combine. Add the meringue-purée mixture to the batter after it is halfway macaroned.

2. Buttercream: If your buttercream has been in the refrigerator longer than 1 hour, whip it using the balloon whip attachment of your stand mixer on medium-high speed until light and fluffy, about 10 minutes. Add the berry purée and a few drops of food coloring (if using) and continue to whip it until fluffy and homogenous, 2 to 3 more minutes.

3. Transfer the buttercream to a piping bag and pipe it onto the bottom of a macaron shell and top with another shell about the same size. Store the cookies in an airtight container in the refrigerator for up to 2 days.

Makes about 20 large cookies

GF, SF

MADAGASCAR-VANILLA MACARONS

Vanilla bean powder is made from vanilla beans that have been processed into flour. If you can't find it commercially, make your own by grinding chopped vanilla beans into a fine powder with a spice grinder.

Macaron Shells
6 tablespoons aquafaba
3 ounces (85 grams) granulated organic sugar
1/4 teaspoon cream of tartar
3.35 ounces (95 grams) almond meal
3 ounces (85 grams) confectioners' sugar
1 teaspoon vanilla bean powder

Vanilla Buttercream
1/2 cup Swiss Buttercream (page 115), freshly prepared or rewhipped
1/2 teaspoon vanilla bean powder

1. Prepare the shells as for Basic Macaron Shells (page 110), following the ingredient amounts listed here, but add the vanilla to the food processor with the almond meal and confectioners' sugar.

2. Prepare the buttercream by combining the Swiss buttercream with the vanilla in a small bowl. Using a spatula, beat the buttercream until it is homogenous.

3. Transfer the buttercream to a piping bag and pipe onto the bottom of a macaron shell and top with another shell about the same size. Store the cookies in an airtight container in the refrigerator for up to 2 days.

Makes about 20 large cookies

GF, SF

SWISS BUTTERCREAM

Swiss buttercream is made by melting sugar and egg whites together before whipping them into a meringue and then adding butter. Typical buttercream is made with sugar and butter and is therefore overtly sweet. Swiss buttercream is loved because the meringue adds a base to the buttercream, making it possible to add less sugar while still maintaining a creamy, fluffy texture. The temperature of the butter is critical in this recipe, since vegan butter is not made of cream and acts differently at different temperatures. If possible, use a thermometer to measure the temperature of your butter.

> 1/2 cup aquafaba
> 3/4 cup granulated organic sugar
> 1 cup (2 sticks) nondairy butter
> 2 tablespoons vegan shortening
> 1/4 teaspoon cream of tartar
> 1 teaspoon pure vanilla extract

1. Combine the aquafaba and sugar in a small saucepan over medium heat. Cook, stirring, until the sugar dissolves. Transfer to a heat-proof container and refrigerate until completely cool, about 6 hours.

2. Chop the butter and shortening into 1-inch cubes and place them on a plate. Bring the butter to about 55°F, slightly colder than room temperature. This should take somewhere between 20 to 30 minutes. Check the internal temperature with an instant-read thermometer.

3. Transfer the aquafaba-sugar mixture and the cream of tartar to the bowl of a stand mixer and, using the balloon whip attachment, whip on medium-low speed for 5 minutes. Increase the speed to medium-high and continue to whip until stiff peaks form (page 5), about 10 more minutes.

4. Add the butter and shortening pieces every 5 seconds while the mixer is on medium-high speed. Add the vanilla; the mixture will break but will recombine again. Continue to whip until the buttercream is smooth and fluffy, an additional 5 to 8 minutes.

5. Use the buttercream immediately or transfer it to an airtight container for up to 1 hour in the refrigerator. If stored longer, the buttercream will need to be whipped again until light and fluffy using medium-high speed for up to 10 minutes. The buttercream will keep for up to 2 weeks stored in the refrigerator.

Makes about 2 cups

GF, NF, SFO

Soy-Free Option: Use a soy-free vegan butter.

CHOCOLATE MACARONS

These macarons start with chocolate shells and are filled with chocolate ganache. Roll the cookies in Cinnamon-Caramel Chocolate Crunch, if desired.

Chocolate Macaron Shells
6 tablespoons aquafaba
3 ounces (85 grams) granulated organic sugar
1/4 teaspoon cream of tartar
3.35 ounces (95 grams) almond meal
3 ounces (85 grams) confectioners' sugar
2 tablespoons (1 gram) unsweetened Dutch-process cocoa powder
2 tablespoons cocoa nibs, optional

Chocolate Ganache
2 tablespoons nondairy milk
1 tablespoon maple syrup
1 teaspoon refined coconut oil
1/2 cup nondairy semisweet chocolate chips
1/2 teaspoon pure vanilla extract
Cinnamon-Caramel Chocolate Crunch, optional (recipe follows)

1. **Shells:** Prepare the shells as for Basic Macaron Shells (page 110), following the ingredient amounts listed here. Add the cocoa to the food processor with the almond flour and confectioners' sugar. If using the cocoa nibs, place 3 to 5 nibs on half the piped cookies after they have been banged on the counter.

2. **Ganache:** Make the ganache by heating the milk, maple syrup, and oil in a small saucepan to a simmer over medium heat or in a microwave. Remove the mixture from the heat and add the chocolate chips. Stir well until the chocolate is melted and the sauce is very smooth. Chill in the refrigerator until the ganache is completely cool. Stir well until fluffy.

3. Transfer the ganache to a piping bag and pipe it onto the bottom of a macaron shell and top with another shell about the same size. Roll the exposed ganache in the crunch mixture, if desired. Store the cookies in an airtight container in the refrigerator for up to 2 days.

|||||||||||||||||||||||||||||||||||||||||||||||||
Makes about 20 large cookies

GF, SF

CINNAMON-CARAMEL CHOCOLATE CRUNCH

1/2 cup granulated organic sugar
1/4 cup bittersweet chocolate chips
1/4 teaspoon ground cinnamon

1. Prepare a silicone mat or piece of parchment paper set on a large baking sheet. Add the sugar to a small saucepan set over medium heat. Cook, stirring constantly, until all the sugar melts and is an amber color; depending on the type of sugar you use, this can take up to 8 minutes.

2. Remove the melted sugar from the heat, add the chocolate chips and cinnamon, and stir until the chocolate is melted. Immediately transfer the mixture to the prepared sheet and spread as thin as you like. Cool completely.

3. Break the caramel into large pieces and transfer to a food processor. Process into small pieces. Sift the pieces using a fine-mesh strainer to remove any chocolate dust. Store the in an airtight container for up to 4 weeks.

Makes about 1/2 cup

GF, NF, SF

ESPRESSO MACARONS

These macaron shells are laced with coffee flavor throughout, and the coffee ganache filling is rich and creamy.

Espresso Macaron Shells
6 tablespoons aquafaba
3.35 ounces (95 grams) granulated organic sugar
1/4 teaspoon cream of tartar
3.35 ounces (95 grams) almond meal
3 ounces (85 grams) confectioners' sugar
2 teaspoons ground instant coffee (grind in a spice grinder)
2 tablespoons cocoa nibs, optional

Chocolate-Coffee Ganache
2 tablespoons nondairy milk
1 tablespoon maple syrup
1 teaspoon refined coconut oil
2 teaspoons ground instant coffee
1/2 cup nondairy semisweet chocolate chips

1. Shells: Prepare the shells as for Basic Macaron Shells (page 110), following the ingredient amounts listed here. Add the espresso to the food processor with the almond flour and confectioners' sugar. If using the cocoa nibs, place 3 to 5 nibs on half the piped cookies after they have been banged on the counter.

2. Ganache: Heat the milk, maple syrup, oil, and espresso in a small saucepan to a simmer, over medium heat or in a microwave. Remove the mixture from the heat and add the chocolate chips. Stir well until the chocolate is melted and the sauce is very smooth. Chill in the refrigerator until the ganache is completely cool. Stir well until fluffy.

3. Transfer the ganache to a piping bag and pipe it onto the bottom of a macaron shell and top with another shell about the same size. Store the cookies in an airtight container in the refrigerator for up to 2 days.

Makes about 20 large cookies

GF, SF

TUILE COOKIES

These delightfully crisp cookies are perfect for serving your dessert in or for garnishing your dessert. They are light and stay crisp for a few hours after they are baked if stored in an airtight container. Use a stencil and an offset spatula to spread the cookie batter, because the cookies have to be uniformly thin for even baking.

 1/4 cup confectioners' sugar
 1/4 cup unbleached all-purpose flour
 1/4 teaspoon psyllium husk powder
 2 tablespoons aquafaba
 1 tablespoon melted nondairy butter
 1 teaspoon pure vanilla extract

1. Sift the sugar and flour together in a small bowl. Whisk in the psyllium husk powder. Add the aquafaba, butter, and vanilla. Stir together into a smooth paste using the whisk. Set the batter aside to rest for 20 minutes.

2. Preheat the oven to 350°F. Using a stencil about 1/16-inch thick, spread the batter on an oiled, parchment-lined baking sheet or silicone baking mat. Remove the template when the batter is spread. Alternatively, use an offset spatula to spread the batter into circles or strips about 1/16-inch thick. Make sure the batter is spread evenly or some portions of the cookie will not bake consistently. Ovens can sometimes have hot and cold spots.

3. Bake the cookies for 5 to 8 minutes, checking for light browning around the edges. Using an offset spatula, remove the cookies from the baking sheet after 10 seconds and form them as needed. Cool the cookie sheet completely before baking more tuiles.

4. To make cups, drape the still-warm cookies over a jar. To make cones, shape the cookies around a cone-shaped foil or other object. To make curls, cut the warm cookies into strips using a pizza cutter (do not cut on the silicone mat) and curl the warm cookies around a wooden spoon.

5. Once cool, the cookies can be used as vessels in which to serve dessert or used as garnishes. The cookies will break down fast as soon as they are filled with wet ingredients, so prepare the dessert right before serving. Store the cookies in an airtight container for up to 4 hours.

Makes about 12 cookies

NF, SFO

Soy-Free Option: Use a soy-free vegan butter.

DUTCH BUTTER COOKIES

||||||||||||||||||||||||||||||||||||||||||||||||||||||||||||||||||||||||||||||||||||||||||||

These delicious crisp cookies are buttery and tender on the inside and crisp on the outside. They remind me of the cookies we used to sell in tins for fundraisers at school. You can shape them using a piping bag or a cookie press.

>   3/4 cup (1 1/2 sticks) nondairy butter, softened
>   1/2 cup granulated organic sugar
>   1/4 cup aquafaba
>   1 teaspoon pure vanilla extract
>   2 cups unbleached all-purpose flour
>   1/2 teaspoon psyllium husk powder
>   1/4 teaspoon sea salt
>   Coarse sugar, optional
>   Shredded coconut, optional

1. Preheat the oven to 400°F. Combine the butter and sugar in a medium bowl. Mix well with a wooden spoon until completely creamed. Add the aquafaba and vanilla and mix well. Add the flour, psyllium husk powder, and salt and mix well until combined uniformly. Transfer the dough to a piping bag fitted with a 1/2-inch tip.

2. Pipe the cookies into desired shapes, about 1/4-inch thick and 2-inches in diameter or length, directly onto baking sheets lined with parchment or silicone mats. Pipe the dough into the shapes of pine trees, wreathes, circles, spirals, or ovals. Sprinkle the cookies with coarse sugar or shredded coconut, if desired.

3. Bake the cookies for 10 to 13 minutes or until they are lightly browning around the bottom edges. The baking time depends on the size and shape of the cookies. Transfer the cookies to a cooling rack to cool completely. Store the cookies in airtight containers for up to 1 week.

||||||||||||||||||||||||||||||||||||||||||||||

Makes 30 to 35 cookies

NF, SFO

Soy-Free Option: Use a soy-free vegan butter.

SUGAR COOKIES

These are the cookies to make if you love decorating with Royal Icing (page 126). They are only lightly sweetened and are ready for the addition of the icing. If you are planning on enjoying them without icing, sprinkle the cookies with granulated sugar before baking and dress up the flavor by adding citrus zest or an extract.

> 1/2 cup granulated organic sugar, plus more for topping
> 1/2 cup Butter (page 10) or store-bought nondairy butter
> 2 1/2 tablespoons aquafaba
> 1 teaspoon pure vanilla extract
> 1 1/2 cups unbleached all-purpose flour
> 1/4 teaspoon baking powder
> 1/4 teaspoon sea salt
> 1/4 teaspoon ground nutmeg, optional

1. Combine the sugar, butter, aquafaba, and vanilla in a medium bowl. Using a hand mixer, blend the mixture until well combined, about 1 minute. Sift in the flour, baking powder, salt, and nutmeg (if using). Blend again until the mixture resembles very wet sand.

2. Form the mixture into a disk or a 7-inch long cylinder, wrap in wax paper, and chill in the refrigerator for at least 1 hour before using. If made into a cylinder, give the dough a roll to even out the flat surface that developed before the dough firmed up.

3. Preheat the oven to 375°F. Remove the dough from the refrigerator and, if it was shaped into a disk, roll it out to a 1/4-inch thickness on a lightly floured work surface if making shaped cookies. Cut the cookies into the desired shapes and transfer them to a baking sheet lined with parchment paper or a silicone mat. Alternatively, if the dough was rolled into a cylinder, slice off 1/4-inch thick pieces and transfer them to the prepared baking sheet. Sprinkle the cookies with additional sugar if not decorating with royal icing.

4. Bake the cookies until the edges are very lightly browned, about 10 to 12 minutes, and transfer the cookies, parchment paper and all, to a cooling rack. This will prevent the cookies from overbaking. After 4 minutes, transfer the cookies directly to the cooling rack. Cool the cookies completely before decorating.

Makes about 25 cookies

NF, SFO

Soy-Free Option: Use a soy-free vegan butter.

Variations: Substitute 1 teaspoon citrus extract or almond extract for the vanilla extract. If adding citrus extract, add 1 teaspoon zest.

Snickerdoodles: Roll small balls of cookies in cinnamon-sugar, flatten them, and bake.

SOFT-BATCH CHOCOLATE CHIP COOKIES

When I was growing up, we could afford few treats, but one my mom would make sure to get for us occasionally was a popular chocolate chip cookie that was crisp on the outside and soft on the inside. I've taken Somer McCowan's Best Vegan Chocolate Chip Cookie recipe (which was inspired by her sister, Holly) and adapted it to make these scrumptious cookies. Thank you, Somer, for the inspiration! Somer is the author of *The Abundance Diet* and blogs at Vedgedout.com.

- 1 1/4 cups unbleached all-purpose flour
- 1/2 teaspoon baking soda
- 1/4 teaspoon sea salt
- 1/2 cup (1 stick) nondairy butter, softened
- 1/2 cup granulated organic sugar
- 1/4 cup packed Light Brown Sugar (page 23) or store-bought light brown sugar
- 1/4 cup aquafaba
- 1 teaspoon pure vanilla extract
- 1 cup nondairy semisweet chocolate chips

1. Preheat the oven to 375°F. Prepare a baking sheet with parchment paper or a silicone mat. Sift together the flour, baking soda, and salt in a medium bowl and set aside.

2. Add the butter, sugar, brown sugar, aquafaba, and vanilla to a medium bowl and, using a whisk or a sturdy spoon, mix together very well. Add the flour mixture and chocolate chips and mix well, until there is no more flour visible. If the dough is too loose, chill the dough in the refrigerator for 15 minutes.

3. Scoop 2-tablespoon portions of cookie dough about 2 inches apart onto the prepared baking sheet. Bake the cookies until golden brown, about 10 to 12 minutes. Bake only one sheet of cookies at a time. Remove the cookies from the oven, cool them on the baking sheet for 3 minutes, and transfer the cookies to a cooling rack. Cool completely before storing in an airtight container for up to 1 week.

Makes 18 cookies

NF, SFO

Soy-Free Option: Use a soy-free vegan butter.

PISTACHIO AND CRANBERRY BISCOTTI

These are the perfect holiday gift. These biscotti are surprisingly easy to make and beautiful to give. They can also be made weeks in advance to avoid the mad rush during the holiday season. You could change up the pistachios with pepitas, swap the cranberries for chopped apricots, or create any number of variations regarding the nuts and fruit. Make these treats extra special by dipping them in Royal Icing (page 126).

    1 3/4 cups unbleached all-purpose flour
    1/2 cup dried cranberries
    1/2 cup chopped shelled pistachios
    1 teaspoon baking powder
    1/8 teaspoon sea salt
    1/4 cup aquafaba
    1/2 cup granulated organic sugar
    2 tablespoons canola or other neutral oil
    1 teaspoon pure vanilla extract
    Royal Icing (page 126), optional

1. Preheat the oven to 350°F. Combine the flour, cranberries, pistachios, baking powder, and salt in a medium bowl and set side.

2. Add the aquafaba, sugar, oil, and vanilla to the bowl of a stand mixer and, using the beater attachment, mix for 1 minute. Add the flour mixture to the sugar mixture in 2 increments and beat until the dough is cleaning the sides of the bowl, 1 to 2 minutes.

3. Transfer the dough to a lightly floured work surface and roll the dough into a 10-inch log. Transfer the log to a baking sheet lined with parchment paper or a silicone baking mat and flatten the log into an 11- x 3- x 3/4-inch rectangle. Bake the rectangle until it is firm to the touch, about 25 minutes.

4. Remove the baking sheet from the oven and allow the biscotto to cool to the touch, about 10 minutes. Transfer the biscotto to a work surface and cut on the bias into 3/4-inch slices. Transfer the slices, cut side down, back to the baking sheet.

5. Reduce the temperature of the oven to 325°F. Bake the biscotti for 8 minutes, flip the cookies, and continue to bake until they are dry and lightly golden, about 8 minutes. Cool the biscotti completely on a cooling rack before icing or storing in an airtight container for up to 6 weeks.

Makes 18 to 20 cookies

NFO, SF

ROYAL ICING

This recipe features four different consistencies of icing to cover all your decorating needs. The most practical and versatile icing is the Decorating Icing, which can act as an outliner or be used to flood a cookie. This icing will dry hard and shiny. Use it to decorate Sugar Cookies (page 122).

  8 ounces confectioners' sugar
  1/8 teaspoon cream of tartar
  3 tablespoons aquafaba
  1/4 teaspoon lemon or pure vanilla extract
  Food coloring, optional
  Water, as needed

1. **Base Icing:** Sift the confectioners' sugar into the bowl of a stand mixer. Add the cream of tartar and mix. Add the aquafaba and mix just to combine. Using a balloon whip, whip the icing on medium-high speed until lighter in color, about 4 minutes. Add the extract and whip for another minute. Add a few drops food coloring (if using) and whip for another minute, until the color is uniform. This makes 1 cup of thick base icing. All icing should be stored tightly covered to prevent hardening. Use the Base Icing as glue to hold gingerbread houses together and other applications where a stiff, sticky food glue is needed. Transfer 1/4 cup of the Base Icing to a small bowl to make one of three royal icings: Outliner, Decorating, or Flooding Icing.

2. **Outliner Icing:** To 1/4 cup base icing, add 1/8 to 1/4 teaspoon plus 1/8 teaspoon water, depending on the amount of extract and food coloring used. Mix gently with a spoon to avoid adding air bubbles. The consistency of the icing should be relatively stiff, dropping off the spoon in blobs. Use this icing to make boarders around cookies.

3. **Decorating Icing:** To 1/4 cup base icing, add 1/4 to 1/2 teaspoon water, depending on the amount of extract and food coloring used. Mix gently with a spoon to avoid adding air bubbles. The consistency of the icing should be relatively thick, flowing off the spoon slowly. A ribbon of icing should melt back into the rest of the icing within 15 seconds. Use this icing to make lines and detailed works.

4. **Flooding Icing:** To 1/4 cup base icing, add 1/2 to 3/4 teaspoon water, depending on the amount of extract and food coloring used. Mix gently with a spoon to avoid adding air bubbles. The consistency of the icing should be relatively thin, flowing off the spoon easily. A ribbon of icing should melt back into the rest of the icing within 6 to 8 seconds; any less and the icing is too thin. Use this icing to cover areas of a cookie within borders that have been drawn using outliner or decorating icing.

5. For best results, use parchment cones to draw lines using the outliner or decorating icing. Cut off a very small piece of the tip of the cone before use. Use a spoon or parchment cones to coat cookies with the Flooding Icing. Use a toothpick or skewer to move icing to tight areas of the cookie or to fix missed spots or remove air bubbles. After flooding a cookie with the icing, give the cookie a good shake (horizontally on a work surface) to distribute the icing evenly. Allow the icing to dry for 24 hours before stacking and storing.

Makes 1 cup Base Icing
GF, NF, SF

AUTUMN-SPICED BREAD PUDDING

This dessert is one of those surprising aquafaba creations. This bread pudding turns out like the real deal, thanks to the combination of bread, aquafaba, and psyllium husk powder. For an amazing version, use Challah bread. It will set like the egg-based version, all the components fusing together into one pudding.

6 tablespoons aquafaba
2 tablespoons melted nondairy butter
1/2 cup granulated organic sugar
2 cups nondairy milk
1 teaspoon psyllium husk powder
1 teaspoon pumpkin pie spice mix or a combination of ground spices (such as ginger, cardamom, cinnamon, nutmeg)
1 teaspoon pure vanilla extract
6 cups (3/4-inch) cubed stale French or Challah bread (page 66)
1 cup dried fruit (such as cherries, raisins, or apricots), coarsely chopped if needed
1/2 cup pecans, walnuts, or pepitas, coarsely chopped
1/4 cup packed Light Brown Sugar (page 23) or store-bought light brown sugar
2 tablespoons rolled oats
1 tablespoon canola or other neutral oil

1. Add the aquafaba to a blender and blend on low speed. With the blender on low speed, add the melted butter in a slow, steady stream. Add the granulated sugar and milk slowly. Increase the speed to medium and add the psyllium husk powder, pumpkin pie spice, and vanilla.

2. Transfer the bread and dried fruit to a 2 1/2-quart casserole dish and pour on the custard mixture. Push down the bread to submerge it in the custard as much as possible and set aside to hydrate for 15 minutes.

3. Preheat the oven to 325°F. Combine the nuts, brown sugar, oats, and oil in a small bowl and mix well. Sprinkle the mixture over the bread pudding and bake for 50 minutes. Remove the pudding from the oven and allow it to cool for 20 minutes to firm up before serving.

Makes 8 servings

NF, SFO

Soy-Free Option: Use a soy-free vegan butter.

MADELEINES

Madeleines, sponge cakes, and génoise cake all spring from the same formula—they are all yolk or whole egg–based cakes that are light and fluffy. Because aquafaba is not a straight yolk replacement, a few adjustments need to be made, but it is possible to create a spongy cake. Both Stefanie Ramsden Dougherty, of GreenSageBlog.com, and I were inspired by the traditional madeleine and have each created our own versions of the small, dainty cakes.

5 tablespoons aquafaba
1/8 teaspoon cream of tartar
6 tablespoons granulated organic sugar
1/2 cup plus 2 tablespoons unbleached all-purpose flour, plus more as needed
3/4 teaspoon baking powder
1/4 teaspoon sea salt
1/8 teaspoon psyllium husk powder
2 tablespoons nondairy butter, melted, plus more as needed
1 teaspoon lemon or orange zest
1 teaspoon pure vanilla extract

1. Add the aquafaba and cream of tartar to the bowl of a stand mixer. Using a whisk, whip the aquafaba for 10 seconds. Using a balloon whip attachment, whip the aquafaba on medium speed for 5 minutes. Increase the speed to medium-high and continue to whip for another 4 minutes, or until the aquafaba forms firm peaks (page 5). Add the sugar, 1 tablespoon at a time, over the course of 3 minutes and continue to whip until the sugar has dissolved, about 4 to 5 more minutes.

2. Combine the flour, baking powder, salt, and psyllium husk powder in a medium bowl. Sift the flour mixture on top of the meringue and drizzle the melted butter on top of the flour. Fold the mixture gently. Add the zest and vanilla and fold again. Chill the batter in the refrigerator for at least 45 minutes before using.

3. Prepare a 12-well madeleine pan or mini cupcake pan by greasing the pan generously with butter. Sprinkle the pan with flour generously and shake off excess flour. Refrigerate the pan while the batter is chilling.

4. Preheat the oven to 400°F. Remove the batter and prepared pan from the refrigerator. Portion about 1 heaping tablespoon of batter into each of the wells of the pan and place the pan in the preheated oven. Immediately reduce the temperature to 375°F and bake for 13 to 14 minutes, or until the cakes are slightly browned on the edges. Cool the cakes in the pan for 3 minutes before transferring them to a cooling rack. Enjoy as soon as possible, as the madeleines are best fresh.

Makes 12 regular-size cakes

NF, SFO

Soy-Free Option: Use a soy-free vegan butter.

CHEWY FUDGE BROWNIES

Rich, chocolatey, and chewy on the inside and lightly crisp outside, these brownies are sure to satisfy any chocolate craving. Make sure to use Dutch-process cocoa powder and bake the brownies just until a test toothpick is still holding onto a few crumbs. The aquafaba acts as an emulsifier and light leavener in this decadent desert. These brownies are also perfect as an addition to any of the ice creams in this book; add about 1 cup chopped brownies during the last minute of churning.

Meringue
1/2 cup aquafaba
1/4 teaspoon cream of tartar
2/3 cup granulated organic sugar
1/3 cup packed Light Brown Sugar (page 23) or store-bought light brown sugar

Fudge Brownie Batter
3/4 cup unsweetened Dutch-process cocoa powder
3/4 cup unbleached all-purpose flour
1/2 teaspoon sea salt
1/2 teaspoon baking powder
1/4 cup neutral canola or other neutral oil
2 tablespoons nondairy milk
2 teaspoons pure vanilla extract

1. **Meringue:** Prepare an 8- x 8-inch square pan with a sheet of parchment paper hanging over one set of opposite sides of the pan to form "handles" for removing the baked brownies later. Preheat the oven to 325°F. Add the aquafaba and cream of tartar to the bowl of a stand mixer. Using a whisk, whip the aquafaba for 10 seconds. Using a balloon whip attachment, whip the aquafaba on medium speed for 5 minutes. Increase the speed to medium-high and continue to whip for another 5 minutes, or until the aquafaba can hold firm peaks (page 5). Add the granulated sugar and brown sugar (add the granulated sugar first and then the brown sugar), 2 tablespoons at a time, over the course of 3 minutes and continue to whip for an additional 2 minutes, or until the sugar has dissolved and the meringue is climbing the side of the bowl.

2. **Batter:** Sift together the cocoa, flour, salt, and baking powder in a medium bowl. Add the cocoa mixture, sifting it again, right on top of the meringue. Add the oil, milk, and vanilla directly on top of the cocoa mixture and macaronage (page 107) the mixture until a pourable batter forms without any obvious air bubbles.

3. Add the batter to the prepared pan and bake the brownies until a toothpick inserted into the middle comes out clean with only a few moist crumbs, about 30 to 50 minutes. Do not overbake (but note that glass baking dishes will need a longer baking time). Run a knife around the edges of the pan and, grasping the overhanging parchment paper, transfer the brownies to a cooling rack. Cool completely before serving.

Makes 12 small brownies

SF, NF

POUND CAKE

Traditionally, the creaming of the butter for such a long time and the use of eggs provide the leavening for this classic cake. Because of the persnickety nature of aquafaba, the addition of a little baking powder is called for in this recipe. Make this recipe using cake flour, as the superfine granules of flour are important in making the texture so tender. These cakes keep their height better if baked in mini loaf tins, but don't let that deter you; this cake is amazing.

    1 cup (2 sticks) nondairy butter, room temperature
    1 cup granulated organic sugar
    8 ounces cake flour
    1 teaspoon baking powder
    Pinch turmeric
    1/2 cup aquafaba, room temperature
    1/4 cup Yogurt (page 18), room temperature, or plain unsweetened store-bought nondairy yogurt
    2 teaspoons psyllium husk powder
    1 teaspoon pure vanilla extract

1. Prepare a 9-inch loaf pan by lining the bottom with parchment paper; grease the sides of the pan that are not covered with the paper. Preheat the oven to 350°F. Check the temperature of the butter; it should be between 65°F and 70°F.

2. Add the butter and sugar to the bowl of a stand mixer fitted with a paddle attachment. Cream the butter and sugar at medium speed until light and fluffy, 8 minutes; it is important to cream the mixture this long to incorporate lots of air into the batter.

3. Sift together the flour, baking powder, and turmeric in a small bowl and set aside. Combine the aquafaba and yogurt in a separate bowl; add the psyllium husk powder and mix well.

4. Add the aquafaba mixture to the butter mixture while the mixer is on medium-low. Add about 1/4 cup at a time and allow the butter to blend well before adding the rest of the aquafaba mixture in increments. Add the flour mixture in the same way, about 1/4 cup at a time, on low speed. Once all the flour mixture is added, add the vanilla and mix for 30 seconds. Transfer the batter to the prepared loaf pan and bake the cake for 1 hour. Check for doneness using a thermometer; the temperature of the cake should be 210°F. If baking in mini loaf pans, bake for 30 minutes and test for doneness.

5. Cool the cake in the pan for 10 minutes before removing it to cool for 10 more minutes on a cooling rack, removing the parchment paper as well. Serve or store in an airtight container for up to 3 days.

||||||||||||||||||||
Makes 1 loaf

NF, SFO

Soy-Free Option: Use a soy-free vegan butter.

BONUS:
BEAN RECIPES

Now that you have created all these amazing aquafaba dishes, you may find yourself with a few batches of chickpeas on hand. This chapter offers a number of creative ways to utilize the cooked beans. The recipes span the globe and the palate. There are four amazing recipes for roasted chickpeas and even a recipe for the popular Ethiopian shiro stew.

Popular Chickpea Recipes

A bonus of using aquafaba is the abundance of chickpeas you will have to use in recipes—and there is no shortage of great ways to cook with chickpeas. In addition to the recipes in this chapter, here is a list of other delicious ways to prepare chickpeas.

- **Chakhchoukha:** Algerian stew of chickpeas and tomatoes, eaten with a semolina flatbread.
- **Chana masala:** Indian chickpea curry.
- **Falafel:** Middle Eastern fried ball or patty of ground chickpeas.
- **Hummus:** Levantine dip or spread made of puréed chickpeas and tahini.
- **Chickpea noghl:** Candied roasted chickpeas dipped in rosewater syrup.
- **Ciceri e tria:** Italian-Arabian fried pasta mixed with boiled pasta and chickpeas.
- **Leblebi:** Spicy or sweet Arabic roasted chickpeas.
- **Msabbaha:** Hummus-style dip that contains whole chickpeas.
- **Minestra di ceci:** Italian chickpea soup.
- **Revithia:** Greek chickpeas baked with onion and rosemary.
- **Topik:** Armenian chickpea balls with potato and currants.
- **Chickpea tagine:** A stew of chickpeas and vegetables that is cooked in a distinct earthenware pot.
- **Chickpea noodle soup:** Chickpeas make a wonderful addition to any noodle soup.
- **Chickpeas and dumplings:** Dumplings cooked in a rich, savory chickpea broth.
- **No-tuna salad:** Chickpeas lend a flaky texture in lieu of tuna in the traditional salad.
- **Minestrone soup:** Chickpeas are a classic addition to this tomato-based soup.
- **Pasta e fagioli:** Another classic Italian soup, this one made with beans and pasta.
- **Buffalo chickpeas:** Cooking the chickpeas in the popular sauce makes for an easy and fast sandwich filling.
- **Chili chickpeas:** Chickpeas are a hearty addition to either the red or green variation of this Tex-Mex classic.

Clockwise from top left: Tourtiere Roasted Chickpeas, Moroccan Merguez-Spiced Roasted Chickpeas, Canary Island Mojo Rojo Roasted Chickpeas, Five-Spice Maple Glazed Roasted Chickpeas.

ROASTED CHICKPEAS FOUR WAYS

||||||||||||||||||||||||||||||||||||||||||||||||||||||||||||||||||||||||||||||||||||||||||||||||||||||||||||||||||||||||||||||

Whether you use these as snacks from a bowl, toss them into a wrap, or sprinkle them on salad, these four varieties of roasted chickpeas will show you how versatile the little legume can be. I provide an Asian version that uses five-spice powder and black bean sauce, a Moroccan version that is spiced like a North African sausage, a version that is precursor to the popular Puerto Rican mojo marinade, and a Canadian version that is a nod to their famous meat pie, the tourtiere. Each version makes about 1 1/2 cups.

Five-Spice Maple Glazed Roasted Chickpeas

> 2 cups cooked chickpeas
> 1 tablespoon plus 1 teaspoon black bean-garlic sauce
> 1 tablespoon maple syrup
> 1 tablespoon rice vinegar
> 2 teaspoons toasted sesame seed oil
> 3/4 teaspoon five-spice powder
> 1/2 teaspoon finely grated fresh ginger

1. Preheat the oven to 350°F. Bake the chickpeas on a baking sheet lined with parchment paper or a silicone mat for 30 minutes.

2. Combine the black bean-garlic sauce, maple syrup, vinegar, oil, five-spice powder, and ginger in a small blender. Blend until smooth.

3. Transfer the partially baked chickpeas to a medium bowl and add the spice paste. Toss well, return the chickpeas to the baking sheet, and continue to bake for another 20 minutes, stirring after 10 minutes. Remove the baking sheet from the oven and allow the chickpeas to cool; they will become crisp upon cooling. If you would like very crunchy beans, bake them for up to another 5 to 10 minutes. Enjoy the cooled chickpeas soon, as they lose their crispiness after a while.

GF, NF

Moroccan Merguez-Spiced Roasted Chickpeas

> 2 cups cooked chickpeas
> 1 teaspoon fennel seeds
> 1 teaspoon coriander seeds
> 1 teaspoon cumin seeds
> 1 1/2 teaspoons paprika
> 1/2 to 1 teaspoon sea salt
> 1/2 teaspoon granulated organic sugar
> 1/8 to 3/4 teaspoon cayenne
> 1/8 teaspoon ground cinnamon

1/8 teaspoon ground black pepper
3 cloves garlic, coarsely chopped
2 tablespoons olive oil
2 tablespoons fresh lemon juice

1. Preheat the oven to 350°F. Bake the chickpeas on a baking sheet lined with parchment paper or a silicone mat for 30 minutes.

2. Add the fennel, coriander, and cumin seeds to a small skillet or saucepan and cook the seeds over medium heat until fragrant and toasted, about 3 minutes. Remove the seeds from the heat, cool for 1 minute, and transfer to a spice grinder or small blender. Grind into a powder. Add the paprika, salt, sugar, cayenne, cinnamon, black pepper, garlic, oil, and lemon juice to the blender and blend into a paste.

3. Transfer the partially baked chickpeas to a medium bowl and add the spice paste. Toss well, return the chickpeas to the baking sheet, and continue to bake for another 20 minutes. Remove the baking sheet and allow the chickpeas to cool; they will become crisp upon cooling. If you would like very crunchy beans, bake them for up to another 5 to 10 minutes. Enjoy the cooled chickpeas soon, as they lose their crispiness after a while.

GF, NF, SF

Canary Island Mojo Rojo Roasted Chickpeas

2 cups cooked chickpeas
1/4 cup coarsely chopped fresh or jarred roasted red pepper
4 garlic cloves, coarsely chopped
2 tablespoons olive oil
2 tablespoons sherry vinegar
1 teaspoon smoked paprika
3/4 to 1 teaspoon sea salt
1/2 to 1 teaspoon cayenne
1/2 teaspoon ground cumin
1/2 cup whole raw almonds or 1/4 cup raw pepitas or a combination

1. Preheat the oven to 350°F. Bake the chickpeas on a baking sheet lined with parchment paper or a silicone mat for 30 minutes.

2. Combine the red pepper, garlic, oil, vinegar, paprika, salt, cayenne, and cumin in a small blender. Blend until smooth.

3. Transfer the partially baked chickpeas to a medium bowl and add the spice paste and almonds or pepitas. Toss well, return the chickpeas to the baking sheet, and continue to bake for another 20 minutes, stirring after 10 minutes. Remove the baking sheet from the oven and allow the chickpeas to cool; they will become crisp upon cooling. If you would like very crunchy beans, bake them for up to another 5 to 10 minutes. Enjoy the cooled chickpeas soon, as they lose their crispiness after a while.

GF, NF, SF

Tourtiere Roasted Chickpeas

2 cups cooked chickpeas
1 medium potato, peeled and cut into 1/2-inch cubes
1 medium carrot, cut into 1/4-inch slices
1/4 cup white wine or 3 tablespoons vegetable broth with 1 tablespoon white wine vinegar
2 tablespoons canola or other neutral oil
4 garlic cloves, coarsely chopped
1 1/2 teaspoons onion powder
1 1/2 teaspoons dried savory or 2 1/2 teaspoons herbes de Provençe
3/4 teaspoon sea salt
1/4 teaspoon celery seeds, optional
1/4 teaspoon ground allspice
1/8 teaspoon ground cloves
1 teaspoon Vegemite (see Note)
1 teaspoon maple syrup, optional

1. Preheat the oven to 350°F. Bake the chickpeas on a baking sheet lined with parchment paper or a silicone mat for 10 minutes. Add the potato and carrot to the baking sheet and continue to bake for an additional 20 minutes.

2. Combine the wine, oil, garlic, onion powder, savory, salt, celery seeds (if using), allspice, cloves, Vegemite, and maple syrup (if using) in a small blender. Blend until smooth.

3. Transfer the partially baked chickpea and potato mixture to a medium bowl and add the spice mixture. Toss well, return the chickpea mixture to the baking sheet, and continue to bake for another 25 minutes. Remove the baking sheet and allow the chickpeas to cool; they will become crisp upon cooling. If you would like crunchy beans and crisp potatoes, bake them for up to another 5 to 10 minutes. Enjoy the cooled chickpeas soon, as they lose their crispiness after a while.

GFO, NF, SF

Gluten-Free Option: Use a brewer's yeast extract paste that is gluten-free or use 2 teaspoons of reduced-sodium tamari and 2 teaspoons of nutritional yeast.

Note: Vegemite is a thick, salty paste that is a leftover product of beer making. It is brewers' yeast extract that has been flavored and spiced. It is readily available at grocery stores in the spice aisle. Check ingredients or contact the individual companies as some are gluten-free and some are not.

ROSEMARY AND ROASTED GARLIC HUMMUS

|||||||||||||||||||||||||||||||||||||||||||||||||||||||||||||||||||||||||||||||||||||||||||||||||||||||||||||||||||||||||||||||||||||||||||||||||||||

Hummus is a favorite go-to when you have extra chickpeas to use up, as can be the case when you get heavily involved with aquafaba. This recipe is a bit unorthodox and just different enough from a classic hummus (a version for that follows this recipe) that you don't feel like you've been there and done that.

> 2 tablespoons olive oil
> 1/2 small onion, coarsely chopped
> 1 tablespoon coarsely chopped fresh rosemary
> 2 garlic cloves, coarsely chopped
> 2 cups cooked chickpeas
> 1 tablespoon tahini
> 1 to 2 tablespoons fresh lemon juice
> 1/4 to 1/2 teaspoon sea salt
> Ground black pepper, to taste
> Water, as needed

1. Heat the oil in a medium skillet over medium heat. Add the onion and cook, covered, until light golden brown, about 6 to 8 minutes, stirring occasionally. Add the rosemary and cook 1 minute. Add the garlic and cook until everything is golden brown, about 2 more minutes. Add the chickpeas to the skillet to warm them through.

2. Transfer the chickpea mixture along with the tahini, lemon juice, salt, and black pepper to a food processor. Process until puréed, 1 to 2 minutes, scraping the side of the bowl as needed. Add 2 tablespoons water and process until smooth, 3 to 4 minutes. Add more water, 1 tablespoon at a time, if needed, to achieve a smooth consistency. Taste and adjust seasoning with salt, black pepper, and lemon juice.

|||||||||||||||||||||||||||||||||||||||||

Makes 4 to 6 servings

GF, NF, SF

Classic Hummus: Warm the chickpeas in a pot of water or in a microwave. Drain well and transfer them to the food processor and add the other ingredients, omitting the onion and rosemary and using raw garlic. Increase the tahini to 2 tablespoons, if desired. Add only enough water to make a smooth purée.

CHICKPEA AND ZUCCHINI FŐZELÉK

Főzelék is Hungary's version of Shiro Wot (page 156) in the sense that it is most often homemade, eaten any time of day, is either the main course or an accompaniment, and is neither a stew nor a soup but somewhere in between. Hungarians make all kinds of vegetables and legumes into főzelék and here I am offering a simple, quick version. It is quite delicious served with the Fasírt Hungarian Burgers (page 54).

1 1/2 cups cooked chickpeas, rinsed and
    drained
2 medium zucchini, finely chopped or grated
1/2 small onion, minced
Vegetable broth, as needed
1 teaspoon sea salt

3 tablespoons olive oil
1/4 cup unbleached all-purpose flour
4 garlic cloves, minced
1 teaspoon Hungarian paprika
Unsweetened plain nondairy milk, as needed
Ground black pepper, to taste

1. Combine the chickpeas, zucchini, onion, broth to just cover the vegetables, and salt in a large saucepan over medium heat. Bring to a boil, reduce to a simmer over medium heat, and cook until the onion and zucchini are tender, about 10 minutes.

2. Heat the oil in a small saucepan over medium heat. Add the flour and garlic and cook, stirring constantly, until the garlic is lightly golden and the flour smells nutty, about 2 minutes. Remove from the heat, add the paprika, and mix well. Add about 1 cup of the cooking liquid from the zucchini mixture and mix well with a whisk. Whisk another cup of cooking liquid into the mixture and transfer all of this mixture to the large saucepan with the zucchini. Mix well and bring to a simmer to thicken the stew.

3. Use an immersion blender to blend the stew to your desired consistency. The stew should just be shy of a purée, with some larger bits of chickpeas and vegetables visible. If it is too thick, add a few tablespoons of milk. Season generously with salt and black pepper. Serve.

Makes 4 to 6 servings

GFO, NF, SF

Gluten-Free Option: Omit the flour. Cook the garlic as directed. Combine 1/4 cup nondairy sour cream with 2 tablespoons cornstarch and mix well. Add to the főzelék right before blending it and bring just to a simmer to thicken.

Variations

- **Green Bean Főzelék:** Omit the chickpeas and zucchini. Use 1 1/2 pounds green beans, trimmed and cut into 1-inch pieces. Increase the cooking time by 5 minutes or until the green beans are tender. Do not purée.
- **Zucchini Főzelék:** Omit the chickpeas and use 3 medium coarsely chopped summer squashes, either zucchini or yellow. Purée lightly.

PERUVIAN ROASTED CHICKPEA-POTATO BOWL

This is an easy bowl to put together since you can marinate the vegetables as long as you need to and have it ready to cook whenever it's convenient. You can also switch out the asparagus for green beans, zucchini, or cauliflower. It really is a delicious and versatile meal.

Marinade
2 tablespoons fresh lime juice
2 tablespoons vegetable broth
4 garlic cloves
1 teaspoon ground cumin
1 teaspoon paprika
3/4 teaspoon sea salt
1/2 teaspoon dried oregano
1/2 teaspoon granulated organic sugar
1/4 teaspoon ground black pepper
8 ounces asparagus, trimmed and cut in half
12 ounces small baby potatoes (about 2-inches in diameter), scrubbed
2 large carrots, cut into 1/4-inch slices
2 1/2 cups cooked chickpeas
2 tablespoons olive oil

Salad
1 small jalapeño chile, seeded and finely chopped
3/4 cup fresh cilantro, loosely packed
1 garlic clove
1/4 cup Mayonnaise (page 16) or store-bought vegan mayonnaise
3 tablespoons Yogurt (page 18) or plain unsweetened store-bought nondairy yogurt
2 to 3 teaspoons fresh lime juice
1 tablespoon olive oil
Salt and ground black pepper, to taste
1 ripe Hass avocado, pitted, peeled, and coarsely chopped
1 medium cucumber, peeled, seeded, and coarsely chopped

1. Make the marinade by combining the lime juice, broth, garlic, cumin, paprika, salt, oregano, sugar, and black pepper in a small blender. Blend until smooth. Add the asparagus, potatoes, carrots, and chickpeas to a medium bowl. Toss with the marinade and set aside for at least 2 hours.

2. Preheat the oven to 375°F. Transfer just the potatoes to a baking sheet and bake for 10 minutes. Add the rest of the marinated vegetables (except the asparagus) and the marinade, and continue to bake for another 25 minutes. Add the asparagus and drizzle the vegetables with the olive oil. Continue to bake until the potatoes are tender, about 10 minutes.

3. Make the salad by combining the jalapeño, cilantro, garlic, mayonnaise, yogurt, lime juice, and olive oil in a blender. Add salt and black pepper to taste. Blend until smooth. Add the avocado and cucumber to a small bowl; add just enough sauce to coat. Taste and adjust the seasoning. Serve the roasted chickpeas and vegetables with the salad and the rest of the sauce.

Makes 4 servings

GF, NF, SF

CURRIED CARIBBEAN COCONUT CHICKPEAS

I offer you a simple homemade curry powder at the beginning of this recipe, because fresh curry powder is superior to one that has been sitting in your pantry; you will notice a difference if you use store-bought curry powder as it lacks the potency and brightness. This curry is also on the sweeter side, in keeping with its traditional Caribbean roots.

Curry Powder
2 tablespoons coriander seeds
1 teaspoon peppercorns
1 teaspoon cumin seeds
1 teaspoon fenugreek seeds
1 tablespoon paprika
1/2 teaspoon turmeric

Curry
3 tablespoons canola or other neutral oil
2 tablespoons Curry Powder (recipe above)
1 medium onion, minced
4 garlic cloves, minced
2 small dried chiles, such as árbol, optional

2 tablespoons tomato paste
4 cups chopped vegetables (e.g., green beans, cauliflower, bell pepper, carrot)
2 cups cooked chickpeas
1 (14-ounce) can coconut milk
1 (15-ounce) can diced tomatoes, undrained
1 1/2 to 2 1/2 tablespoons granulated organic sugar
3/4 teaspoon sea salt
1/2 teaspoon ground black pepper
Cooked rice, for serving
Fresh cilantro, for garnishing, optional

1. **Curry Powder:** Heat the coriander seeds, peppercorns, cumin seeds, and fenugreek seeds in a small skillet over medium heat. Cook until the seeds smell toasted, 3 to 4 minutes, stirring. Remove from the heat and add the paprika and turmeric. Transfer the mixture to a spice grinder (or a small blender or coffee grinder) and process into powder. Cool completely and store in an airtight container for up to 3 months.

2. **Curry:** Heat the oil in a large skillet over medium heat. Add the curry powder and cook for 1 minute. Add the onion, garlic, and chiles (if using), and cook until the onion is beginning to turn golden, 3 to 4 minutes. Add the tomato paste and cook for 1 minute. Add the vegetables, chickpeas, coconut milk, diced tomatoes, sugar, salt, and black pepper. Mix well, bring to a boil, reduce to a simmer over medium heat, and cook until the flavors are melded and the sauce thickens considerably, 25 to 30 minutes, stirring occasionally. Taste and adjust the seasoning with salt and sugar. Serve with hot cooked rice and garnished with cilantro (if using).

Makes 4 servings

GF, NF, SF

FALAFEL DÖNER

||||||||||||||||||||||||||||||||||||||||||||||||||||||||||||||||||||||

Döner is the precursor to the roasted meat sandwiches shawarma and gyro, mainstay meals of the Middle East. For me, it wasn't too much of a stretch to use falafel in place of the meat and make it into a sandwich inspired by the traditional döner. These patties are a nod to all three popular Mediterranean sandwiches—falafel, shawarma, and gyro—but contain no lemon or lemon juice, a typical addition to all three in some form. Use gluten-free panko or breadcrumbs and a gluten-free flatbread to make this gluten-free.

1/2 cup panko breadcrumbs
1/4 cup vegetable broth
1 teaspoon psyllium husk powder
4 tablespoons olive oil, divided
1 medium onion, coarsely chopped
4 garlic cloves, minced
1 teaspoon dried parsley
1/2 teaspoon dried oregano
1/2 teaspoon dried rosemary
1/2 teaspoon sea salt

Ground black pepper, to taste
2 cups cooked chickpeas

For Serving
Toom Sauce (page 17) or Rosemary and
    Roasted Garlic Hummus (page 141)
Lavash or pita bread, warmed
Pickle slices
Onion or tomato slices
Hot sauce

1. Combine the panko, broth, psyllium husk powder, and 1 tablespoon of the oil in a small bowl. Mix well and set side. Oil a baking sheet with 1 tablespoon of the oil and set aside. Preheat the oven to 350°F.

2. Heat the remaining 2 tablespoons oil in a medium skillet over medium heat. Add the onion, garlic, parsley, oregano, rosemary, salt, and black pepper. Cook, stirring, until the onions are golden brown, about 10 minutes. Add the chickpeas and continue to cook until the beans are starting to brown, about 3 to 5 minutes. Transfer to a food processor.

3. Process the mixture into a coarse purée. Add the panko mixture and pulse to combine. Divide the mixture into 6 portions. Form the portions into 1/2-inch thick oblong patties and place them on the oiled baking sheet. Spray or brush the patties with more oil. Bake the patties until crisp and slightly firm, 30 to 40 minutes, flipping the patties halfway through. Once baked, the patties will continue to firm up as they cool.

4. To serve, spread the toom sauce or hummus on the warmed bread, add a falafel patty, pickles, and onion and tomato (or any combination of the accompaniments). Add hot sauce if desired and serve.

||||||||||||||||||||||||||||
Makes 6 patties

GFO, NF, SF

KOREAN DAK GALBI

Dak galbi translates to *chicken ribs,* but since the original dish doesn't contain anybody's ribs, there is no reason not to make this without chicken, too. Chickpeas are perfect in this Korean sauté and you'll be surprised at how the aromatic marinade can be used in so many variations. After you've made it once, feel free to use seitan, tofu, mushrooms, or other vegetables in place of the chickpeas. The Korean rice cakes (yuki toppogi) are extremely popular and are eaten sautéed with oil, added to soups, or added to dishes such as this. The cakes are made from pounded and steamed glutinous rice flour, which adds a delightful chew to the stir-fry. Although traditional to include them because of their unique texture, they can be omitted if necessary.

2 tablespoons gochujang (red pepper paste)
2 tablespoons reduced-sodium tamari
2 tablespoons rice wine or dry vermouth
1 tablespoon toasted sesame seed oil
4 garlic cloves, minced
1 tablespoon granulated organic sugar
2 teaspoons Curry Powder (page 145)
1/2 teaspoon ground ginger
2 cups cooked chickpeas
1 (7-ounce) package baked tofu, cut into
   1-inch cubes, or 1 additional cup cooked
   chickpeas, rinsed and drained
2 tablespoons canola or other neutral oil
1/4 teaspoon fennel seeds

2 small sweet potatoes (about 3 ounces each),
   peeled and cut into 1/2-inch wedges
1 small onion, cut into 1/4-inch wedges
1 (150-gram) package Korean rice cakes,
   soaked in hot water 10 minutes
3 cups chopped cabbage
1 cup loosely packed basil leaves, coarsely
   chopped
1/2 cup loosely packed mint leaves, coarsely
   chopped
Cabbage leaves, for serving
Cucumber slices, for serving
Toasted sesame seeds, for serving

1. Combine the gochujang, tamari, wine, sesame oil, garlic, sugar, curry powder, and ginger in a shallow 8- x 8-inch pan. Mix well and add the chickpeas and tofu. Set aside to marinate for as little as 15 minutes to up to overnight. If marinating overnight, bring to room temperature before cooking.

2. Heat the oil in a large skillet over medium heat. Add the fennel seeds and cook for 20 seconds. Add the sweet potatoes, onion, and rice cakes. Cook until the rice cakes and sweet potatoes begin to color, about 10 minutes. Add the chickpeas and tofu with all the marinade, the cabbage, basil, and mint. Stir well to combine. Cook, stirring occasionally, until the cakes begin to develop a crust and the vegetables are tender, 10 to 15 minutes. Serve in cabbage leaves with cucumber slices and sprinkled with sesame seeds.

Makes 4 servings

GF, NF, SFO

Soy-Free Option: Omit the tamari. Add 2 tablespoons coconut aminos and 1/4 teaspoon sea salt.

CHICKPEA GULYÁS

||||||||||||||||||||||||||||||||||||||||||||||||||||||||||||||||||||||||||||

I am Hungarian, and I must include a recipe for a Hungarian dish in all my books. This is a very traditional and popular dish that very often gets the wrong treatment when veganized. In keeping with the original, the only thickener in this Gulyás is natural reduction of the sauce. This is not Gulyás soup but is the sauté or stew that I grew up with. Cooking the chickpeas for so long mellows out the flavor and texture that so often overwhelms other dishes. Serve this with Galushka (page 49) and an acidic cucumber and tomato salad for a complete Hungarian meal.

3 tablespoons olive oil, divided
1 large onion, minced
6 garlic cloves, minced
2 cups cooked chickpeas
1 small tomato, coarsely chopped
1 1/4 teaspoons sea salt
1 teaspoon granulated organic sugar
1 tablespoon Hungarian paprika
1 teaspoon smoked paprika
4 cups vegetable broth, divided
1 medium potato, cut into 1/2-inch dice
1 medium carrot, cut into 1/4-inch slices
Ground black pepper, to taste
1/4 cup minced fresh parsley

1. Heat 2 tablespoons of the oil in a large skillet over medium heat. Add the onion, garlic, and chickpeas. Cook, stirring occasionally, until golden brown, 12 to 15 minutes. Add the tomato, salt, and sugar and cook for another 2 or 3 minutes.

2. Remove the skillet from the heat, add the remaining 1 tablespoon oil, Hungarian paprika, and smoked paprika. Stir well, add 2 cups of the broth and return to the heat. Bring to a boil, reduce to a strong simmer over medium heat, and cook until most of the broth is reduced, about 10 minutes.

3. Add the potato, carrot, and the remaining 2 cups broth and cook until the sauce thickens and the flavors are melded, 15 to 20 more minutes. Season with black pepper and taste and adjust the seasoning with salt. Garnish with the parsley and serve with pasta or galushka (page 49).

||||||||||||||||||||||||||||||||||||||||||

Serves 4 with a side

GF, NF, SF

Galushka (top, page 49) with Gulyás (opposite)

PULLED SEITAN CHICKPEA ROAST

Chickpeas added to gluten create a texture that is unique and delicious. Adding mashed chickpeas interferes with the gluten threads from forming and makes it possible to "pull" the seitan apart into small chunks. On the flip side, because of this unique attribute, the roast has to be handled a little more gingerly when being flipped and removed from the pot and even then some small parts of the roast will begin to unravel. It is well worth the effort. I offer you this recipe, which can be used in other "pulled" recipes, and a home-style Memphis barbecue feast (page 154) to use the roast in. All the components can be made individually or together, all at once or in stages—it's really up to you.

   3 tablespoons nutritional yeast flakes
   1 teaspoon sea salt
   1/2 teaspoon onion powder
   1/2 teaspoon garlic powder
   1/2 teaspoon dried sage
   1/2 teaspoon dried thyme
   1 1/4 cups well-cooked chickpeas
   1 cup plus 3 tablespoons vital wheat gluten flour, stirred before measuring
   8 3/4 cups vegetable broth, divided

1. Add the nutritional yeast, salt, onion powder, garlic powder, sage, and thyme to a small blender or spice grinder. Blend into a fine powder and add to a large bowl or, what I prefer to use, a stand mixer fitted with a paddle attachment. Add the chickpeas to a food processor and pulse 4 to 6 times, until there are no whole beans remaining. Add to the large bowl. Add the gluten to the large bowl and 3/4 cup of the broth. Mix well and knead for 4 minutes or until gluten threads form; some pieces of chickpeas will fall out of the gluten. Shape the gluten into an oblong roast or one that will fit into your slow cooker.

2. Heat the remaining 8 cups broth in a slow cooker over medium or high heat until warm. Add the roast, cover the slow cooker, and cook on low (or medium, if your cooker has the option) for 5 hours until cooked through. If using the Instant Pot, cover the pot with a regular lid, not the sealing lid that comes with it. Allow the roast to cool completely before removing it from the slow cooker and using it.

Makes 1 (1 1/2-pound) roast

NF, SF

MEMPHIS-STYLE PULLED BARBECUE

Pulled Seitan Chickpea Roast (page 153), cooled
2 tablespoons canola or other neutral oil
1/4 cup Dry Memphis Rub (page 155)
1 cup ketchup
1/2 cup molasses
1/3 cup apple cider vinegar
1/4 cup yellow mustard
2 tablespoons Worcestershire Sauce (page 23) or store-bought vegan Worcestershire sauce
1 garlic clove, minced
Ground black pepper, to taste
Sea salt, to taste
Cayenne, to taste

1. Gently squeeze most of the moisture out of the seitan roast. Rub the roast all over with the oil and then sprinkle evenly with the rub. Massage the rub into the roast. Transfer the roast to a baking dish lined with parchment paper and set aside for 1 hour at room temperature.

2. Preheat the oven to 400°F. Bake the roast for 15 minutes, flip, and bake for another 15 minutes, or until the roast is heated through and the surface is beginning to brown. Set aside to firm up and cool for 10 minutes.

3. While the roast bakes, make the sauce by combining the ketchup, molasses, vinegar, mustard, Worcestershire sauce, garlic, black pepper, salt, and cayenne in a medium saucepan. Cook over medium heat until the sauce comes to a simmer, reduce the heat to medium-low, and cook for 15 minutes.

4. Use a fork to shred the roast as desired for a barbecue plate or sandwiches. Serve with the sauce.

Serves 4 to 6

NF, SF

DRY MEMPHIS RUB

||||||||||||||||||||||||||||||||||||||||||||||||||||

1/4 cup paprika

2 tablespoons smoked paprika

2 tablespoons packed Light Brown Sugar (page 23) or store-bought light brown sugar

2 tablespoons garlic powder

1 tablespoon onion powder

1 tablespoon sea salt

1 tablespoon ground black pepper

1 tablespoon chili powder

1/2 to 2 teaspoons cayenne

1 1/2 teaspoons ground cumin

1 1/2 teaspoons dry mustard

Combine the paprika, smoked paprika, brown sugar, garlic powder, onion powder, salt, black pepper, chili powder, cayenne, cumin, and mustard in a small bowl. Mix well and store in an airtight container for up to 4 weeks.

|||||||||||||||||||||||||||||||||

Makes about 1 cup

GF, NF, SF

SHIRO WOT

I have been a huge fan of Ethiopian food ever since Kittee Berns, author of *Teff Love,* released her first 'zine many years ago. Although very easy to prepare, shiro wot cannot be rushed as the spices in the berbere need to be cooked properly. It might seem that there is too much liquid in the beginning, but the wot will thicken as it cooks and the extra liquid makes allowance for the added moisture to evaporate and cook the stew properly. Serve the wot with flatbread or injera, if you have it, and a green salad dressed with a simple vinaigrette or the Italian Dressing on page 20.

Note: Before making this recipe, the Shiro Flour needs to be made well in advance because it needs time to dehydrate.

> 1 large onion, grated
> 1/4 to 1/2 cup canola or other neutral oil
> 8 garlic cloves, minced
> 2 medium tomatoes, coarsely chopped
> 4 cups water
> 3/4 cup Shiro Flour (page 158)
> Sea salt and black pepper, to taste
> Injera, pita, or lavash, for serving
> Steamed vegetables, for serving, optional
> Sliced jalapeño chile, for serving, optional

1. Add the onion to a medium saucepan and cook over medium heat until the onion is dry, about 8 minutes. Add the oil and garlic and cook until the onion is beginning to brown. Add the tomatoes and cook until they have broken down, about 5 minutes. Add the water and bring to a boil.

2. Using a whisk, blend in the Shiro Flour gradually. Simmer the wot over medium heat, stirring occasionally, until it thickens and the flavors meld, 45 to 55 minutes. Taste and adjust the seasoning with salt and black pepper.

3. Serve with your choice of injera, pita, lavash, or steamed vegetables and sliced jalapeño.

Makes 4 servings

GF, NF, SF

SHIRO FLOUR

|||||||||||||||||||||||||||||||||||||||||||||||

Shiro wot is a smooth stew eaten in any Ethiopian household for breakfast, lunch, or dinner. Shiro also refers to the legume flour from which shiro wot is made. Shiro flour can be made using up to six different dried legumes, but here I've kept it simple with just two. The beauty of shiro wot, besides being a singularly delicious dish, is that once you make the flour, preparing the wot (or stew) is quick and easy.

Note: Making the flour in advance will make preparing the Shiro Wot (page 156) an easy convenience. Although the flour takes a while to dehydrate it will keep well for months.

> 2 cups dry yellow split peas
> 6 cups water
> 1 (stamp-size) kombu, optional
> 3 cups cooked chickpeas, rinsed and drained
> 6 tablespoons Berbere Powder (recipe follows) or store-bought berbere powder
> 2 teaspoons sea salt

1. Combine the peas, water, and kombu (if using) in a large saucepan over medium-high heat. Bring to a boil and reduce to a simmer over medium heat. Cook the peas, partially covered, until tender, about 1 hour, adding more water as needed. Alternatively, pressure-cook the peas for 3 to 7 minutes (depending on the size and age of the peas), allowing for natural release. Remove and discard the kombu.

2. Drain the peas well and transfer them to a baking sheet lined with parchment paper or a silicone mat. Transfer the chickpeas to a separate baking sheet lined with parchment paper or a silicone mat. Bake the legumes in a 250°F oven (no need to preheat) for 3 hours, or until thoroughly dried out; the chickpeas will need additional baking as outlined in the next step.

3. Transfer the chickpeas to a blender and blend into a coarse grind, starting the blender on low and increasing the speed gradually, scraping the side of the jar as needed. Return the chickpeas to the baking sheet and bake for an additional hour.

4. Transfer the peas to the blender and blend into a very fine powder, as directed for the chickpeas. The grind should feel very fine when the flour is rubbed between your fingers. Transfer to a bowl and grind the chickpeas the same way when they are done baking. Add the berbere powder and salt to the chickpeas and blend well to combine. Add the chickpea powder to the pea powder and use a whisk to mix well.

5. Sift the flour though a very fine mesh strainer to remove any large pieces. Either blend these pieces again or compost them. Cool completely, transfer the flour to an airtight container, and store for up to 6 months in a cool, dry place.

|||||||||||||||||||||||||

Makes 3 cups

GF, NF, SF

BERBERE POWDER

2 teaspoons coriander seeds
1 teaspoon fennel seeds
1/2 teaspoon peppercorns
1/4 cup paprika
1 tablespoon onion powder
2 teaspoons sea salt
1 teaspoon to 1 tablespoon cayenne
1/2 teaspoon ground cardamom
1/2 teaspoon ground ginger
1/2 teaspoon ground cinnamon
1/4 teaspoon ground nutmeg
1/8 teaspoon ground cloves
1/8 teaspoon ground allspice

Add the coriander seeds, fennel seeds, and peppercorns to a small skillet and cook over medium heat until the seeds smell toasted, about 3 to 4 minutes. Cool slightly and add to a spice grinder (or a small blender or coffee grinder). Add the paprika, onion powder, salt, cayenne, cardamom, ginger, cinnamon, nutmeg, cloves, and allspice. Grind very well. Sift, if desired, and transfer to an airtight container. The spice will keep for up to 3 months stored in a cool, dry place.

Makes about 1/2 cup

GF, NF, SF

Berbere Oil

Combine 1 tablespoon canola or other neutral-flavored oil with 1/2 to 1 teaspoon berbere powder. Use to garnish the shiro wot (page 156).

INGREDIENTS AND EQUIPMENT

This chapter explains the special ingredients and procedures used in this book. Although you may be already familiar with many of the ingredients, it is worth reading this chapter because I impart additional information that you may find helpful. I also cover some of the special equipment that I encourage you to work with as well.

Ingredients
Equipment
Special Procedures

Ingredients

Agar: A type of seaweed that gels liquids when it is completely dissolved and cooked to a certain temperature. Agar is best when it is bloomed first, soaked in a cool liquid. Citrus interferes with its gelling properties if not dissolved first.

Almond meal: This meal is finely ground almonds. The one from Trader Joe's is perfect for making milk but not for making macarons, since it is not made from blanched almonds. Honeyville Blanched Almond Flour is super finely ground and is perfect for macarons.

Baking powder: Use double-acting baking powder that is aluminum free.

Black salt, kala namak: This is also known as Indian black salt. It is an Indian spice that brings an eggy flavor to recipes.

Cake flour: This is bleached, finely ground wheat flour that makes baked goods very tender. It has the least protein of all the wheat flours.

Chickpeas: These legumes produce the strongest, most stable aquafaba.

Coconut cream: This is coconut milk but without all the water. If you cannot find coconut cream, place a can of full-fat coconut milk in the refrigerator for 1 hour and scoop off the coconut cream that has solidified.

Coconut oil: Use refined coconut oil in this book's recipes, as it has little to no coconut flavor to interfere with the final product.

Coconut milk: Use canned coconut milk, not coconut beverage, which is a completely different ingredient. Coconut milk comes in reduced-fat and regular varieties. Use only the full-fat variety.

Cocoa, unsweetened Dutch-process: This is alkalized cocoa powder. It is lighter in color and tastes milder than natural cocoa.

Cornstarch: Whether using cornstarch or arrowroot in these recipes, after the starch is added (in a slurry), cook it only long enough to thicken; otherwise, the sauce may break.

Cream of tartar: This is a by-product of wine making. It is an acidic ingredient that helps stabilize meringues and break sugar molecules into fructose and glucose.

Extracts: Use extracts that are alcohol-free and as pure as possible.

Flour, gluten-free: Properly measuring all flours is important, but it is especially important for gluten-free flours such as chickpea, sorghum, tapioca, and so on. Fluff the flour by stirring it well with a knife and then use a large scoop to add flour to your measuring cup. Level off the flour using the back of a butter knife.

Glucose/invert syrup: These are also known as cane syrup and corn syrup (not high-fructose corn syrup). These are different kinds of sugar molecules that interfere with sucrose molecules to help prevent crystallization of syrup. They also keep ice crystals from developing in ice cream.

Gochujang: Korean hot red pepper paste.

Kappa carrageenan: This extract from red seaweed is an emulsifier, stabilizer, and gelling agent.

Kombu: This seaweed is used to tenderize beans, among other delicious uses.

Lactic acid: This is an organic acid that is produced by soured milk products, such as yogurt. When purchasing, make sure to buy one that is certified vegan.

Miso: Miso is fermented soybeans and comes in a huge variety of flavors. The flavors are based on the fermentation length and sweetness of the miso. Light or white miso is sweeter and milder because it is fermented for a shorter period of time. Chickpea miso is a soy-free version of miso and preferable for the taste of the cheeses in this book.

Nutritional yeast: This is deactivated yeast that adds umami to dishes.

Oats, rolled and quick: Oats are gluten-free grains. I use them as thickeners and stabilizers in these recipes. Make sure to only use quick oats when directed.

Oil: Unless specified, use a neutral-flavored oil for these recipes. Some of these recipes have very low flavor profiles and need as little added flavor as possible. Even some neutral-flavored oils, such as grapeseed and sunflower seed oil, will impart those flavors to the final product.

Paprika, Hungarian: Hungarian paprika is the best. Popular brands are Szeged and Kalocsa. There are two varieties, sweet and hot. The sweet version is the all-purpose one to acquire.

Pepitas: Pepitas are pumpkin seeds, and they have one of the highest protein contents of plant-based foods. They are also nut-free and delicious.

Psyllium husk powder: This is a type of soluble, dietary fiber that cannot be absorbed by the intestines. It has been used for centuries as a natural digestion remedy. In combination with aquafaba, it makes an adequate yolk replacement in certain recipes. Use the powder form as that has the best texture. If you can only acquire the husk form, blend it into a powder and sift before storing it.

Soymilk: Use soymilk that is made of only soybeans and water. Westsoy Organic Unsweetened Plain is one such brand. Its protein content is 9 grams per serving and makes wonderful yogurt, among other dishes.

Sugar, granulated organic: Use organic sugar (as that is vegan) that is the lightest color and smallest grain that you can find that is closest to regular white granulated sugar. The color is important for the cooking of sugar syrup and the grain is important for dissolving in meringue.

Tahini: This is ground sesame seed paste. It is used in hummus.

Tamari: The recipes in this book were developed using reduced-sodium tamari. If you use regular tamari, your recipes might be much saltier.

Vital wheat gluten flour: This is protein-rich flour that is derived from wheat flour. It is used to make seitan.

Yeast, dry active: This is yeast that gives rise to baked goods. It is best stored in the freezer and activated with warm liquid first to make sure it is viable. See Proofing dough (page 166).

Yogurt: Homemade yogurt is best, but for some applications store-bought soy or coconut yogurt is also good. I'm sure there are some great almond varieties on the market now, but be sure you like the taste and texture before using it in a recipe.

Xanthan gum: This is a thickener and stabilizer that is derived from bacteria.

Equipment

Candy thermometer: A digital one that clips onto the side of your pot is preferable. The range should be 75°F to 450°F.

Dehydrator: An optional appliance. One that can be switched to only use the fan is preferable.

Ice cream maker: If you are making ice cream, an ice cream machine with a 1 1/2-quart bowl that is set in the freezer before use is preferable. To store the ice cream, I recommend mini cups (about 6 ounces each) because the less the ice cream is thawed and refrozen, the better its texture will be.

Immersion blender: These blenders make it easy to prepare mayonnaise, butter, and even comes in handy when blending anything in a pot, such as soup. Acquire one that has a head that can fit inside a wide-mouth mason jar, such as the Cuisinart Smart Stick.

Instant Pot: This home appliance has a stainless steel interior pot and acts as a slow cooker, pressure cooker, steamer, and rice cooker. It is preferable to acquire one that is also a yogurt maker: the 7-in-1 Instant Pot. Other brands are on the market with similar features, but this particular brand is also a yogurt maker.

KitchenAid stand mixer: A stand mixer is absolutely helpful when whipping aquafaba into meringue. The bowl of your stand mixer should be stainless steel and your balloon whip should be large enough to be effective but small enough that it will not interfere with hot sugar syrup when making candy.

Kitchen scale: Truly a valuable piece of equipment in the kitchen. They are relatively inexpensive and save tons of frustration, guesswork, and time. Acquire one that measures in both metric and English systems, because the metric is more accurate since grams are more finely defined than ounces.

Linen nut bag: This is a nut-milk bag that is woven tightly and traps most of the curds or almond meal and allows mostly whey (or milk) to pass through, making for less waste and better texture in the yogurt or nut milk. My favorite is IQzeens Nut Milk Bag, which is made of organic cotton and hemp fibers.

Oven thermometer: Because of the low temperatures that aquafaba meringue needs to be cooked at, for macarons and meringue cookies, an oven thermometer is essential. This economical device will take the guesswork out of baking and ensures success.

Plastic: I tried to limit the use of plastic in this book. Instead of plastic wrap to cover bowls or proof bread, use wax paper, a large dinner plate, or another bowl turned upside down. To wrap candy or pie dough to chill, use wax paper and a rubber band. Use mason jars to store butter and mayonnaise and use a reusable piping bag for macarons and doughnuts. When at all possible, rinse and reuse any plastic wraps or bags.

Strainer, fine-mesh: This is the strainer that is best for rinsing quinoa, so you might already have one. It is also important for sifting confectioners' sugar, cocoa, flour, and almond meal for macarons.

Vitamix: This is a high-speed blender that makes blending nuts and seeds very easy and creates a smooth texture.

Special Procedures

Agar, whipped: Once agar is whipped, such as in the Lemon Meringue Pie (page 90), Marshmallows (page 82), or Coconut–Key Lime Cream Pie (page 95), it is important to not whip it again once you have stopped whipping. Once there is no motion (or when the temperature reaches a certain degree) the agar will start to set. Once it starts to set, if the mixture is disturbed, the lattice work will have been interrupted and your meringue will deflate.

Blending: It is always best to start blending on low speed to break up the ingredients being blended. Increase the speed of the blender as the ingredients get smaller, until you can speed up the blender to maximum speed. If there is not enough liquid in the blender the blades can pull down a large air bubble and suspend any further chopping. When this happens, change the speed of the blender and move the base up and down (or use a tamper) to move the air bubble up and out of the liquid.

Boiling: When liquid boils, the liquid bubbles constantly and vigorously.

Candy-making: See page 74.

Emulsifying: Begin by blending the aquafaba until foamy and frothy. With the blender on medium speed, very slowly add the oil, almost drop by drop. Once the first few tablespoons of oil are added, the emulsification should have occurred and the rest of the oil can be added a bit faster. You can also increase the speed by another quarter speed. Cold oil emulsifies much better because it counteracts the heat from the blender. Coconut oil can only be at room temperature, however, since it will solidify at colder temperatures. In addition, when adding coconut oil, the aquafaba must also be at room temperature; otherwise, the oil will not emulsify but solidify as soon as it hits the cold aquafaba.

Folding: Folding is a process of mixing where a large spatula cuts through the middle of the ingredients in a bowl, and the ingredients are lifted up and over the rest of the mixture. The bowl is turned a quarter and the process is repeated until the mixture is as homogenous as is needed.

Macaronage: See page 107.

Nuts, blending: Nuts are easiest to blend if soaked overnight, but they can also be blended easily if they are first blended with the liquid called for in the recipe then allowed to hydrate for 10 to 15 minutes before blending again until perfectly smooth. Add only about the amount of liquid as there are nuts since blending is much easier when the nuts can break each other. If there is too much liquid, the nuts have more room to get away from one another and this makes it more difficult to blend easily and smoothly.

Nuts, straining: Use a linen or hemp nut-milk bag for the smoothest nut milk. Although it is more challenging to use than a mesh nut-milk bag, it removes more of the pulp. Add only about 2 cups milk to the bag at a time to make it easier to massage the bag to extract the liquid.

Piping: Use a reusable piping bag, a parchment cone (for Royal Icing, page 126) or a zip-top plastic bag with a corner cut off for piping doughnut batter, macarons, or buttercream. Use a tip if so desired.

Proofing dough: When proofing your dough be sure to proof long enough to double the dough but not too long. A proof that lasts too long will result in a baked good that has odd surface texture and not enough rise in the oven. If you can poke your finger into the dough about 1/2-inch and it leaves an indentation that fills in slowly it is perfectly proofed. If you poke it and nothing happens it needs to proof longer (an additional indication here is the size of the dough), if the dough deflates when you poke it then it is over proofed. The exception to these guidelines are gluten-free doughs.

Sautéing: Sautéing is cooking in fat or very little liquid to brown and caramelize ingredients.

Simmering: Simmering is cooking just below boiling temperature. For the recipes in this book, unless otherwise specified, keep the temperature around medium heat.

Yogurt, straining: Straining yogurt removes most of the whey from yogurt. Homemade yogurt (page 18) strains very well and can be made into homemade cheese, but there are commercial brands of yogurt (especially of the coconut variety) that does not strain at all. In addition, note that if coconut yogurt is used, it can also impart a coconut flavor to the final product.

Resources

Amazon.com: Find small appliances, nut-milk bags, finely ground almond flour, and most any pantry-stable ingredient you need to make the recipes in this book.

Grocery store or health food store: Find fresh ingredients and produce, sugar, dried chickpeas, and so on at these local stores.

Trader Joe's: Find most fresh and pantry-stable items here, including almond meal for making Homemade Almond Milk (page 15) and coconut cream for making pies and ice cream. Most also carry Westsoy Organic Unsweetened Plain brand soymilk.

Local regional grocers: These specialty grocery stores (such as Korean, Indian, Japanese, and so on) carry specialty ingredients such as black salt, agar, and gochujang. They also carry pots, pans, and other household equipment.

FrontierCoop.com: Become a wholesale member to receive huge discounts on pantry staples and cooking and baking necessities, such as parchment paper and silicone mats, herbs, spices, and agar.

ModernistPantry.com: This online company sells vegan lactic acid, kappa carrageenan, and cheese molds.

Costco: This bulk store offers refined coconut oil, organic sugar, nuts, and other pantry items at some locations.

Roundup of the "Vegan Meringue — Hits and Misses!" Group

No book on aquafaba would be complete without a shout-out to the group that made it possible for us to come together from around the world to share our successes—and some misses—in aquafaba exploration. Truly, it is this collaboration that made it possible for aquafaba to be the resounding success it is today. Joël and Goose discovered something fantastic, and because we were able to share and learn from each other's experiences, aquafaba has more and more successes every day.

Below is a sample of the recipes that have been posted to the Facebook group and I encourage you to go, join, jump in, start cooking, begin sharing, and continue collaborating with each other. I thank Joël, Goose, the admins of the Facebook group, and all the members that made—and still make—it possible to so easily and so quickly share.

The recipes are available on the Facebook group under the "Files" section. The names in parenthesis are the blogs or sites where the author of the recipe posts regularly. Not all authors have personal sites, but most are active in the Facebook group. Sometimes it is easier to simply head to the author's website or blog (if available) and search for the desired recipe to easily locate it.

Angel Food Cake: Moira Wright

Banana Ice Cream: Natalie Creed (Miso Coco)

Banana Pancakes: Shannon Plush

Belgian Waffles with Yeast: Shosanna Frishberg-Isso

Birthday Cake Macarons: Lacey Siomos (Avocados and Ales)

Black Bean Chocolate Chip Brownies (Gluten-Free): Jacqueline King (The Feel Good Kitchen)

Blueberry Cornbread Cake: Jenny Dunklee (The Lazy Vegan Baker)

Blueberry Muffins: Somer McCowan (Vedged Out)

Brazilian Cheese Bread (Pão de Queijo): Hannah Kaminsky (BitterSweetblog)

Breakfast Pancakes: Anja Vecchi

Carrot Muffin Cakes: Sarah de la Cruz (Fried Dandelions)

CFC Drumsticks (Cruelty-Free Chicken): Zac Bird (Zacchary Bird)

Cheddar Cheese: Lacey Siomos (Avocados and Ales)

Cherry Pie: Sarah Peter-Hamill (Soy Division)

Chocolate and Lemony Sponge Cake: Guy Mugrabi (Everyday Vegan Cooking)

Chocolate Chocolate Chip Cookies (Gluten-Free): Ellen Blonder

Chocolate Crinkle Cookies (Gluten-Free): Heather O'Leary (Vegan Is The New Black on Facebook)

Chocolate Midnight Cake: Rebecca August

Chocolate Sponge Mousse Cake: Faye Baklavops (Veganopoulous)

Choux Pastry: Alyse Marie Houghton

Cinnamon Rolls: Richa Hingle (Vegan Richa)

Cinnamon Walnut Swirl Challah: Stefanie Ramsden Dougherty (Green Sage)

Coconut Macaroons: Siobhain Pembroke Klawetter

Cornbread: Kristy Cutsforth (The Home Cookin' Vegan on Facebook)

Custard (Vegan Galaktoboureko): Faye Baklavops (Veganopoulous)

Genoise Cake: Karolina Tegelaar (Swedish Vegan on Facebook)

German Cinnamon Cookies (Zimtsterne) (Gluten-Free): Anna Siepert

Hummus, Oil-Free: Ania Marcinowska (Lazy Cat Kitchen)

Italian Meringue Buttercream: Linda Julien (Geeky Cakes)

Lazy Samoas: Lacey Siomos (Avocados and Ales)

Lemon Meringue Pie: Skye Michael Conroy (The Gentle Chef)

Mini Crumb Cakes (like Drake's Coffee Cakes): Linda Julien

Mississippi Mud Cake: Kia H. Hansen

Neapolitan Stuffed Easter Bread (Casatiello): Emilia Leese (Emi's Good Eating)

Nougat: Sheri Hutchings

New York-Style Cheesecake: Pamela Myles

Old-Fashioned Egg Nog: Mark Silver

Oreo Macarons: Charis Mitchell (Floral Frosting)

Pancakes (Gluten-Free): Holley Blossom

Pasta: Nathan Kozuskanich (Vegan Dad)

Pavlova: Katrina Stuart (Open Sauce Vegan/Plantified)

Peach Gelato: Rebecca Coleman (Cooking By Laptop)

Pecan Pie: Lex Barnard

Peppermint Mocha Brownies: Sarah De la Cruz (Fried Dandelions)

Pizelle: Genevieve Patchell

Plum and Blueberry Clafoutis: Lisa Le (The Viet Vegan)

Sandwich Bread (Gluten-Free): Janice Mansfield (Real Food Made Easy on Facebook)

Scones: Maria João Furtado

Snickers-Like Bars: Linda Julien

Souffle: Kike Juric Bareta

Sriracha Mayo: Ania Marcinowska (Lazy Cat Kitchen)

Strawberry Cheesecake: Rose Pitts (Sweet Asylum Bakery and Treats on Facebook)

Tuile Cookies: Lucy Parr (Lucy's Friendly Foods)

Vanilla Cake: Rebecca August

Vanilla Mini Donuts: Julia Hammar

Yorkshire Pudding: Charis Mitchell (Floral Frosting)

Acknowledgements

This book had a life of its own. There were moments that were inspiring, moments that I was awestruck, and moments I was almost ready to give up, but knowing how important this book was going to be for the people and the hens, I knew I had to keep going. So, again I washed out my mixer bowl, threw another two batches of chickpeas in the slow cooker and kept at it, many times from early morning to late at night. My hope is that you, like me, will find all the effort and work beneficial to your diet and lifestyle, because ultimately it is the most beneficial to the hens, as anyone who has researched just a tiny bit into the egg industry knows.

Cookbook writing is not a solo affair and this one makes that even more abundantly clear. I want to thank the inspired work of Joël Roessel and Goose Wohlt, without whom none of this would be possible. I'd like to thank the moderators and contributors of the Facebook group *Vegan Meringue – Hits and Misses,* who keep learning, experimenting, and sharing.

I am thankful to my wonderful recipe testers who, again, jumped on board and many even acquired stand mixers of their own solely for the testing—you guys are more awesome than you will ever know. The testers are the reason why these recipes work universally well in all kitchens, not just my own. I can't thank you enough: Kelly and Mac Cavalier, Dorian Farrow, Liz Wyman, Jenna Patton, Russell Patton, Jael Baldwin, Ruchama Burrell, Nichole Kraft, Kip Dorrell, and my dear friend Susan Van Cleave. I am also incredibly appreciative of late-coming testers who jumped into the deep with both feet and completed testing the final round; thank you, Eve-Marie Williams, Darlene and Chris Bruce, and Daneen Agecoutay. It would take pages of this book to detail the help that these folks provided and how they kept the momentum of aquafaba going. They truly made this book possible.

I am also very grateful to Jon Robertson and the team at Vegan Heritage Press. Developing, writing, and testing the recipes are only the first steps. Then the mismatched pieces have to be assembled and turned into a beautiful work of art. You guys are amazing.

I am also grateful to my home-based team: my children, Catt, Katelyn, and Mikel, and my ever-dedicated husband, David. Love you guys!

The book you hold in your hands is due to the diligence and talent of all these behind-the-scenes players. I thank each and every one of you!

About the Author

ZSU DEVER has been involved in the restaurant business most of her life. She hails from a long line of culinary professionals and restaurateurs. She is the author of *Vegan Bowls* and *Everyday Vegan Eats* (also published by Vegan Heritage Press) and blogs at *Zsu's Vegan Pantry*. Zsu is a passionate vegan and resides in San Diego, California, with her three children, three adopted felines, and her husband.

Website: www.zsusveganpantry.com

Facebook: https://www.facebook.com/zsuzsanna.dever

Facebook: https://www.facebook.com/ZsusVeganPantry

Facebook: https://www.facebook.com/EverydayVeganEats

Facebook: https://www.facebook.com/VeganBowls

Twitter: https://twitter.com/ZsuDever

Pinterest: http://www.pinterest.com/zsudever/

Instagram: http://instagram.com/zsus_vegan_pantry

YouTube: https://www.youtube.com/channel/UCyJeCNbFTNSHaPDdK7Y6VgA

Index

W

Y

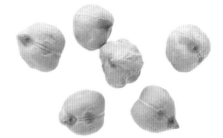

Metric Conversions and Equivalents

The recipes in this book have not been tested with metric measurements, so some variations may occur.

LIQUID	
U.S.	METRIC
1 tsp	5 ml
1 tbs	15 ml
2 tbs	30 ml
1/4 cup	60 ml
1/3 cup	75 ml
1/2 cup	120 ml
2/3 cup	150 ml
3/4 cup	180 ml
1 cup	240 ml
1 1/4 cups	300 ml
1 1/3 cups	325 ml
1 1/2 cups	350 ml
1 2/3 cups	375 ml
1 3/4 cups	400 ml
2 cups (1 pint)	475 ml
3 cups	720 ml
4 cups (1 quart)	945 ml

GENERAL METRIC CONVERSION FORMULAS	
Ounces to grams	ounces x 28.35 = grams
Grams to ounces	grams x 0.035 = ounces
Pounds to grams	pounds x 435.5 = grams
Pounds to kilograms	pounds x 0.45 = kilograms
Cups to liters	cups x 0.24 = liters
Fahrenheit to Celsius	(°F - 32) x 5 ÷ 9 = °C
Celsius to Fahrenheit	(°C x 9) ÷ 5 + 32 = °F

WEIGHT	
U.S.	METRIC
1/2 oz	14 g
1 oz	28 g
1 1/2 oz	43 g
2 oz	57 g
2 1/2 oz	71 g
4 oz	113 g
5 oz	142 g
6 oz	170 g
7 oz	200 g
8 oz (1/2 lb)	227 g
9 oz	255 g
10 oz	284 g
11 oz	312 g
12 oz	340 g
13 oz	368 g
14 oz	400 g
15 oz	425 g
16 oz (1 lb)	454 g

OVEN TEMPERATURE		
°F	Gas Mark	°C
250	1/2	120
275	1	140
300	2	150
325	3	165
350	4	180
375	5	190
400	6	200
425	7	220
450	8	230
475	9	240
500	10	260
550	Broil	290

LENGTH	
U.S.	Metric
1/2 inch	1.25 cm
1 inch	2.5 cm
6 inches	15 cm
8 inches	20 cm
10 inches	25 cm
12 inches	30 cm